ASTROLOGY

COMPATIBILITY AND
YOUR MISSION IN LIFE

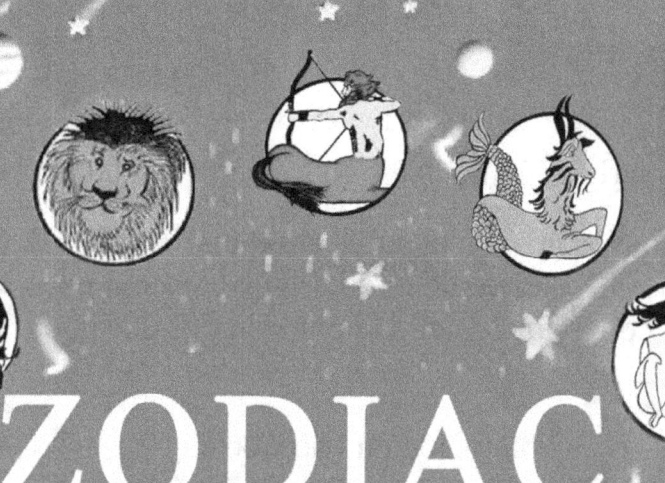

ZODIAC
SIGNS

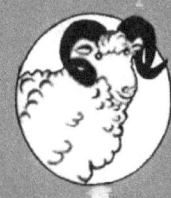

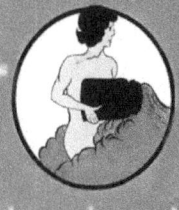

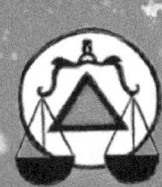

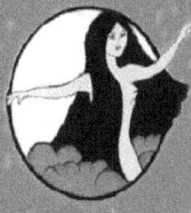

HANNE KLEIN

Astrology

The Zodiacs Signs In Great details

By Hanne Klein

Follow me on Facebook

https://www.facebook.com/theastrologycentre

Table of content

Introduction To The Zodiac Signs

Welcome to my Astrology book on the twelve individual astrological Sun Signs. Thank you so much for downloading it. I'm sure you will not be disappointed. We will first take a journey through each of the Sun Signs and your special mission in life before we go into the compatibility of the signs. Some individuals enjoy good relationships at an awe-inspiring level of personal happiness, while others lead to nothing but disagreement and tragic unhappiness. Why do you have an immediate rapport with one person at first sight, and for no special reason, someone else turns you off, and may even oppose you?

The secret of compatibility has always intrigued people. However, astrology, the oldest science known to man, can provide many answers to the question of this mystery. I have written a detailed explanation of the characteristics of each Sun Sign, also called zodiac sign or star sign.

A Sun Sign on its own is never complete without the full information about the Moon and the planets and where they are positioned in your personal horoscope. But even this shortened kind of analysis of the Sun Signs can tell a great deal about the personality of a person. It can also reveal how the Sun Sign of two different people relates to each other. Before examining the many possible combinations of the twelve Sun Signs, let us look at some of the primary traits of each sign, because they will play an important role in determining compatibility when two people get together in a close relationship.

Astrology is an interesting topic for everyone to learn. It will help you to develop a better understanding of yourself and the people around you. The astrological horoscope is mainly about you and how you get on with people close to you. It can teach you to build a richer and happier life for yourself. Now you are probably thinking, how do I get to know myself better by using astrology? You can use it as a guide whenever you are in doubt about choosing a correct path, and when faced with an important decision, it can point you in the right direction. Astrology is an excellent tool that teaches you about your gifts, talents, and the path you are best suited to follow. When you truly know yourself, you will attract the things just right for you. It can show how you can direct your life and get as much out of life as possible and have a full and rewarding lifestyle.

The horoscope is a chart or diagram representing the positions of the Sun, Moon, planets, the astrological aspects, and sensitive angles at the time of an event, such as the moment of a person's birth. The Sun travels through the twelve signs of the zodiac once a year and stays approximately a month in each sign. The sign the Sun was traveling through when you were born is your Sun sign. In astrology we refer to the Sun and Moon as planets. The Sun is the most powerful planet and has the strongest influence in your astrological chart. The house the Sun was placed in at the time of your birth will influence your unique personality and the way you will go about achieving your goals.

There are two more power points in the horoscope, which have a strong impact on your character. The first is the sign on the ascendant, which is on the cusp of the first house, and the second is the sign the moon was in at the time of your birth. There are twelve Sun Signs in a horoscope, one for each month. It is important to familiarize yourself with the characteristic of each sign because we have all the twelve signs in our horoscope. If there is a sign we don't feel comfortable with, it will be a good idea to get to know it better and analyze yourself to see what it is you feel uneasy about. Or, if you know a person born under that particular sign, recognize that you have that sign, too, in your chart, even though it may be a small part of your makeup.
Ask yourself *"what do you need to learn from this other person so you can feel more at ease in that area of your life."*

Start out by taking small steps to find out what you need to learn. Once you find out why certain things about the other person bother you, get a notebook and write down this question, *why is this person bothering me?* Then write down your response and keep on asking the same question until you get an answer you can connect with. You will be surprised what comes up in the end and it may have nothing to do with the other person, he/she is only acting as an innocent instrument in healing you.

Learning about the zodiac signs will be an interesting journey I promise you. It will take you into many different areas of life you can explore and understand better. You can discover how you can heal yourself in many ways through astrology. You can usually find a solution to your problems by using astrology. The more you know about your own astrological chart the easier it will be for you to see what is going on in your chart. Is there a negative planetary aspect at work in your chart at the moment, if so, then it may not be a good time to start certain things, like a new project.

Before we go any further, I would like to point out that in this book we only talk about the Sun Signs. A personal horoscope would need to be drawn up for you to learn more about your deeper self.

Aries

Aries is a fire sign and is ruled by the planet Mars. It is the ruling sign of the first house of the horoscope. The key word for this sign is 'Action" or new beginning. People born under this sign usually are frank, loyal, and straight forward. They love to start something new. They get very excited about beginning a new project. They are the pioneers of the zodiac and are never happier than when they can start a new venture. They are very adventurous people. They want to get started as soon as possible. In fact, they can't wait to get on with it. If it is not started right away, they could loose interest. Aries enjoy a challenge. If they have something to conquer, it is right down their alley and you will see them shine.

Aries have the quality of leadership and they can make wonderful, inspirational leaders. They have the ability to inspire interest and enthusiasm in others. However, if they have to follow, or are in a situation where they are bossed around by others, they can become discontented and down in the dumps. They are happiest when they are in charge. They feel really good in that position. Basically, they are quick and decisive, both in their actions and in the way they think.

Aries are really good at manifesting their great ideas. However, not every Aries is developed enough to handle their talent as a leader. Many Aries may need to learn what it means to be a good, responsible leader. They may need to learn to think before they speak, and ask themselves this question: *If I make this decision, what effect will it have on the other people?* As a leader Aries should inspire other people to go for their goals and then lead them until they have achieved success.

When Aries does a job they like to get it done swiftly and efficiently and they will not put up with people who are slow to make a decision. If someone gets in their way or tries to stop them from working on their project, they are likely to get annoyed or even aggressive. Don't interfere in their business. They will not appreciate it, because they are very independent and have a fiery, untameable spirit.

This is a dynamic energy, there is nothing sweet and loving about Aries. This energy is about action. It is intended to shake you up and get you out of your comfort zone. A lot of people want to be safe and secure, so they settle for being mediocre. The trouble with that is you don't get in touch with who you are deep inside. You don't live up to your full potential or get to experience how great you can be.

A good time for anyone to tune into this energy is in the month of April as it is ruled by Aries. This month it is time to let go of old things, the state of affairs that is no longer working. Aries destroys the old, outworn ways and ideas, only to build up something new. It is a time to start some real fun and passionate adventure. The reason old things don't work anymore is because Aries has passed that energy frequency and has moved on to a new and more advanced level of energy.

Taurus

Taurus is an earth sign and is ruled by the planet Venus, which bestows Taurus with charm, gentleness, kindness and loyalty. It rules the second house of the horoscope, which has to do with finances and security. The key word of this sign is '*I have*'. People born under this sign place great importance on physical, financial and emotional security. They are not pioneers like their neighboring sign Aries. They are the settlers of the zodiac. They represent good, solid, caring people. Taureans are the practical people who will nurture the unique ideas that were created in Aries and finish them. Taurus is usually conservative, someone who prefers fact and reality rather than fantasy. They are not the ones to build castles in the sky, so to speak. They are doers, not dreamers, and do not scatter their energy, but conserve it, and they try to look at everything from a practical point of view. Taureans are good natured people who set high standards for themselves, but they need to realize it is not everyone who can live up to their expectations. They have to accept people as they are and bear in mind that human relationship is a two-way street. Like a mirror, it is a reflection of oneself.

Taurus at times can be downright stubborn and can have some very fixed ideas about how things should be done. But if Taurus combines that trait with its conservative nature, they can limit themselves and miss some valuable experiences that will allow them to grow. Taurus needs to be careful not to crush its initiative in trying out new enterprises and narrowing its chances for a successful outcome. Sometimes it is good for the soul to take a chance. They usually take their time to make up their mind, but once they decided on a plan they will be very determined to carry it through, come rain, hail and high water.

Taureans have a kind and affectionate nature, and are hardly ever in a bad mood. They do not get easily upset. But they have trouble understanding temperamental volatile, unpredictable people. They like to feel settled and secure. They should always rely on their good nature and patience in their relationships, because that will help keep the genuine, loyal friends they so strongly desire. Taurus likes plenty of space and does not like to be fenced in. This sign rules the month of May so take advantage of this energy during this month, because it can give you the courage to break free from controlled energy. The thing is, we permit others to control us so they will accept us, and we hold ourselves back because we are worried we are not good enough.

If you have your own personal horoscope drawn up for you, then check it out and see which house Taurus is occupying in your chart. That will give you an idea of which energy is influencing your unique personality and the way you go about working towards your goals. Maybe now that you have the awareness of how Taurus influences you, it can help you to feel less uptide.

Gemini

Gemini is an air sign and its ruling planet is Mercury. The key word for this sign is *'I Think'*. It rules the third house of the horoscope, which governs communication. Gemini is all about communication. They love to chat with others and share interesting ideas. They bring life into a conversation. They enjoy making contact with new acquaintances and are really good at building bridges between people. Geminis are incredibly good with words and can talk their way in and out of any situation. They are quick to come up with answers to whatever questions happen to come up during a conversation. Mercury, its ruling planet, bestows this sign with a brilliant, ingenious, and versatile mind. Geminis may not be deep thinkers, but they certainly are clever and very capable.

Gemini rules the nervous system and they can be very restless and have a need to be busy all the time. They have an active mind and should learn to relax and calm themselves. Geminis can also be highly strung, excitable, and enjoy variety and a change of scenery. That could lead them to try many diverse aspects of life.

Gemini is known as the twin sign. It is influenced by two different individualities. One side of its nature is kind, loving and sympathetic towards others, but on the other hand, emotionally, it may not be so deep. It may appear as if the intellectual side steps in and takes a logical approach to things.

Gemini is usually fast and it seems like it can be in two places at once. Here now, and the next minute you are gone. Gemini is fluent in speech and writing. Because of their quick wit, we often find them as script writers or writing for commercials or even small stories. Later in life they might even settle down as authors and write novels or short novellas.

Every Sun Sign has a different energy, and the purpose of this energy is to educate us in a loving way and to transform us to a higher state of mind. Gemini has a wonderful, loving energy and can see beauty in almost anything. However, they are more likely to be lightheartedly affectionate than deeply emotional and intensely passionate. They like to share their affection with many people.

Gemini can usually see two sides to every question, and end up seeing the good in everything. They must learn to discriminate, and see right from wrong, then say, I recognize there is a problem and it needs to be fixed. They bring order so we can see beauty, but the blind spot of this energy is a tendency to ignore problems.

Geminis are adaptable and find little difficulty in adjusting to variety and change of new scenery. They actually thrive on such things. Because of their constant desire for change, it will be unusual for them to go through life and not changing their business, career, or profession at least once or maybe even more often. Their flexible hands and multi talented mind are their one of their greatest assets.

CANCER

Cancer is a water sign and its ruling planet is the Moon. The key word for this sign is *'I Feel'*. It rules the fourth house of the horoscope, which is about the Mother, the home, and family. As far as Cancer is concerned, a house is not a home before you make it into one and let your family feel at home there. If any conflict should occur in the household, then Cancer will worry itself sick until the harmony is back in the home. Cancer has this wonderful, caring, and mothering energy about them. They are excellent at communicating with the people around them, and because of their highly developed intuitive gift, they will pick up on the feelings of others. They can feel if something is wrong with any members of the family and will lovingly try to help or fix the problem. However, they must be careful not to get into the trap of making others too dependent on them and for not to become co-dependent on anyone.

Cancer has a very sensitive and impressionable nature and feels things deeply. They will give up their own interest or the development of their talents, putting their family before themselves and catering to their needs before their own. They tend to worry a lot, and if anyone says or does some hurtful things to them, which is what happens here in life, they will brood about the situation for a long time. Cancers are inclined to store up memories, whether good or bad, and will never forget about the past. They can appear to be shy or apprehensive, and in love they are very sentimental. Patience and persistence are two of they're strong points. When they first decide upon a goal, they will show an incredible determination to reach it.

They sense the way other people feel. and if they are having any problems or are in a difficult situation, they will always be there to give sympathy. Cancer has a strong, instinctive urge to support and protect the ones they love, but if their relationships don't work out, they become moody and very emotional. Their feelings frequently run away with them. It may be wise to try to look at the facts rather than always be guided by your feelings. This might also be a healthier course of action.

Cancer energy is great for communication. So, the month of July, which is ruled by Cancer, is a good time to resolve any issues you have with family and especially your parents. We will keep on creating the same situations with other people until we have resolved any old and deep seated matters with our parents. But we need to be graceful about the way we go about our communication with them. Use compassion, and say to yourself, if I communicate this, what will be the effect on the other person? That way you become sensitive to the other person's feelings with less chance of hurting them.

LEO

Leo is a fire sign and it is ruled by the Sun. The key word for this sign is *'I Will'*. It rules the fifth house in the horoscope. This is the regal sign of the zodiac, and these people have an intense drive toward self-realization. Self-expression is important to them. They are individuals who like to stand on their own and think for themselves. Leos like to be the center of things and will flaunt the flamboyant side of their nature, just to get everybody's attention. Most Leos desire nothing more than to be liked - loved - respected and admired. They want the approval of others. They really have a need to be accepted. It's important for Leos to learn self-approval, for that is the key to this energy. When approval comes from within you, one doesn't need outside recognition

Leo's will think big and cannot stand small-mindedness of any kind. Leo likes to be in charge, and loves to organize and control the current state of affairs. They possess an instinctive power for leadership. As a result, they inspire confidence and admiration in other people because they sense their strength of purpose in other and their tremendous capacity for achieving their goals. This sign is about power, enthusiasm, and determination and has the energy of the will.

They enjoy the good life, romance, entertainment, and having fun with their children. Leos are usually easy-going people, however, they may sometimes blow up, but the anger passes quickly, and immediately afterward, they are sorry and apologetic for having lost their temper.

Leos are warm-hearted and generous and always eager to assist others less fortunate. However, there are times when they do a good turn for others just to attract their admiration and affection which they need so much. In some cases, this is not appreciated. People sense when the right intention isn't behind the service they offer. Every now and then Leo likes to brag about himself, showing off or maybe even be pushing forward to be noticed.

Leos don't fancy second place. They are not happy in a minor position for long, whatever their speciality. They are loyal, sincere, frank and honest persons, but others will often hurt or try to take advantage of them. They love, beauty, and luxury, and have a wonderful sense for arranging parties. They love to entertain in a lavish way. Leos will do best if they are the boss or in a position of authority and responsibility. However, once a Leo develops and opens up his or her mind, they usually possess the ability to research and find creative solutions to problems. And when they have found the answer to the troubles, they can turn around and teach and lead others.

Leo rules the month of August. This will be a good time to take advantage of this powerful energy, which can sometimes be very controlling, whether or not you are a Leo. Take a look at yourself during this time and see if there are any areas in your life where you could be healed from the stress of being too controlling or if someone is trying to control you.

VIRGO

Virgo is an earth sign and its ruling planet is Mercury. The key word for this sign is *'I Analyze'*. It rules the sixth house of the horoscope, which is basically concerned with work, health and service to others. Virgo likes perfection, and they will try their hardest to make things perfect. These people can be very analytical and like to pay attention to all the little details. They will become critical if everything is not close to perfection. They are practical people, but they also possess a keen mind that detects everything that needs improving.

Neatness and attention to details are some of Virgos strong points, but some Virgos may take it too far and become over fussy. Some people from the other signs have the ability to come up with some great idealistic vision, but they need someone practical to put form to their big ideas. This is where Virgo comes in. They can recognize the vision and carry out their ideas on the physical plane. This energy is a total service to humanity. Virgo is earth energy, which means dealing with the physical aspect of things. This energy is also very much about caring for the physical body. Remember, it is the sign of perfection, and in order to care for the body and make it pure, you have to get rid of all the toxins in the body, and not eat anything that can poison it. One of the most important things for Virgo is to stay healthy, to look at nutrition and make sure to get the right food, so the body can maintain a good physical condition and be a pure temple for the soul to reside in. When the body is pure and free of all toxins, it becomes lighter and you attract a much higher energy that will put you on your right path.

Virgo has intellectual brilliance and is a great conversational talent. They like to analyze every situation, and they have an intense love of details in everything they do. They are the epitome of common sense and typically plan far ahead in all aspects of life. However, they can sometimes be too critical and get caught up in worrying too much about the small things and not see the forest for the trees. They need to let go and try to focus on the bigger picture. They will shun the limelight if it brings them into close contact with too many people.

They are even tempered people and violent emotions may either upset or even possible revolt them. Fair criticism of others is fine, but they have to be careful not allow constant faultfinding to spoil their relationships and associations. Everyone can use the month of September, which is ruled by Virgo, to take a look at themselves whether they are Virgos or not. On a scale from one to ten, analyze yourself to find out how you rate when it comes to criticism both of yourself and others. If you are not rating well, then go on a criticism fast during the month of the Virgo energy. Change the negative thoughts you may have to some more positive ones.

LIBRA

Libra is an air sign and the ruling planet is Venus. The key word for this sign is *'I Balance'*. It rules the seventh house of the Horoscope, which relates to relationships, mainly on a one to one basis, like marriage and any close companionship. It can also relate to business and partnership. The Libra energy has to do with relating to others and these people constantly think in terms of the other person. They are brilliant communicators and often act as mediators between people because they are the peacemakers of the zodiac. They need peace and harmony in their surroundings and in personal relationships. They find conflicts and quarrel upsetting. Libras tend to weigh things in any situation, either for or against, because they can see both sides. Therefore, while they might hesitate to arrive at a decision, it is only because it is important for them to find the right balance.

Tact and diplomacy are their strong points and people find them easy to get along with. They know how to serve other people and meet their needs on an emotional level. Libras do not like to hurt other people's feelings and would rather keep quiet, even if it means hurting themselves, just to keep the peace. Venus, the planet of love, which is your ruling planet, bestows Libra with a charming and charismatic nature. They love and appreciate beauty, comfort, luxury, and all the good things life can offer. They gain a lot of pleasure from sharing beautiful things with someone they love. Libras prefer to share with someone and do not like to be alone for too long.

Most Librans enjoy the world of art and are usually talented people with strong artistic abilities that should be developed as it is a great outlet for their creative talents. In the work area, Librans need to be less easy-going, more serious and determined if they want to attain their goals. They must accept the necessity for hard work, along with charm and sparkle. Libra is very much male energy versus female energy, and a true peacemaker will end up with male-female energy and be able to bring it into equality, and not favor one side over the other. The most important energy to be at peace with is always the opposite of your own sex. Libra strives to be in balance.

The month of October is ruled by Libra. If there is anything in your life you need to bring into balance, then you can use this month's energy whether you are a Libra or not. Venus is the ruling planet of this month and this is a good time for working out money situations. Money is considered one of the biggest areas of disagreement. So in order to learn how to handle money, we need to find the conflict in ourselves. Librans often have inner conflict caused by emotional feelings on the one hand and intellectual consideration on the other hand. Money is something Librans must learn to manage. Money has to do with self-worth, self-esteem and it's very much an energy tied up with love.

SCORPIO

Scorpio is a water sign and the ruling planet is Pluto. The key word for this sign is *'I Desire'*. It rules the eight house of the horoscope, which refers to giving birth to something new and letting go of the old, it is about transformation. A Scorpion is someone with tremendous drive, determination and an intensity, which they instill into every part of their life, whether it's work, play or love. They are never satisfied with half measures, because for Scorpio it's all or nothing. They hold a fascinating, irresistible, seductive, and mysterious air about them. Scorpio's energy refers to emotional, intense, deep feelings. They possess a high degree of physical magnetism and many of the opposite sex find themselves attracted to them. They have the ability to implement a strange fascination over other people who happen to tune into their wavelength.

Where love is concerned, emotional intensity, passion, and desire are specific qualities. Scorpios can be quite possessive and feel they own their partners, body and soul. But unless they choose a person who feels flattered by this, they can suffer from jealousy and unhappiness. Scorpios will demand a lot of themselves and expect the same from others, but need to realize other people may not be able to live up to their expectations.

The purpose of the Scorpio energy is like a total deciding point in someone's evolution, because the Scorpio's search for identity is a real one. They will go through major transformations in their lives. They have gone through the other Sun Signs in the past and arrived at Scorpio, and it's always a test, whether they will go for the soul or personality. This is a very advanced energy. There are two sides to this sign; one side is into the personality and wants to try more things and have more experiences in life. Scorpio has always been given the symbol of the Eagle. They fly high above everything, and that is the other side of this energy. It is the advanced side, the higher more spiritual side, reaching out and tuning into the soul.

Scorpio people are extremely sensitive and very intuitive. Their insight to others is rare. They can usually see the truth about people, and through the most elaborate and camouflaged facades. In the month of November, which is ruled by Scorpio and the powerful planet Pluto, we are influenced by a strong emotional intensity. If you have never learned to show your feelings, then this month is an excellent time to learn. You can use this energy whether you are a Scorpio or not. It's very important to express your emotion with this energy, because if you don't, it will go behind a wall and turn into resentment.

Successful business people learned long ago to use this irresistible energy of Scorpio. They discovered that for them to sell their product, they must make it look presentable and so desirable that people cannot resist it; it is the secret to making them want to buy the item. That is how people get caught in this energy, it can be so seductive it pulls people in. However, we have to learn to discriminate and decide for ourselves if we need another experience or if we are able to let the glamour go, and reach for the higher spiritual choice of the soul.

SAGITTARIUS

Sagittarius is a fire sign and the ruling planet is Jupiter the planet of luck and good fortune. The key word for this sign is *'I See'*. It rules the ninth house of the horoscope. Which governs higher learning, long distance travel, law, religion and philosophy. The people born under this sign are the happy go lucky people of the zodiac. They are, cheerful, optimistic, good-natured people. These outgoing, friendly people like to socialize, and because of their delightful sense of humor, they make a lot of friends. Friendships and pleasant human relationships are very important to them. Sagittarius is the sign of expansion, which plays a big part in their lives. These people are the visionaries who have the ability to see the bigger picture in a situation. When some of their friends are in trouble or are stuck with a problem they have difficulty solving, Sagittarius will help them to focus on a more cheerful side of everything.

They are independent people and don't like any kind of restriction or limitation. They enjoy the outdoors and open spaces where they can feel free to explore new places. The Sagittarius sense of humor is among their most endearing traits. They are a high-spirited and friendly, gifted conversationalist.

Sagittarius is a born entertainer and a wonderful storyteller. People love to be entertained. This sign also rules the higher mind. Sagittarians are the teachers, as well as great leaders who get out in front and make fun as they guide people and make them laugh in the process. Through story telling and entertainment they can inspire people to open up their minds to greater awareness. They can also be frank and outspoken because they are honest by nature and come straight to the point. This makes them easy to deal with, because other people don't need to wonder whether they are sincere or not. However, as a result of their frankness, they sometimes put their foot in it and then must try to work their way out of the situation. They don't mean to hurt people's feelings, but simply don't know how to beat around the bush.

Sagittarius loves to take chances, because they are confident that their optimistic attitude will bring good luck in the future. A long distance journey comes under the ninth house, anything to do with travel is right down Sagittarius's alley. They make an excellent travel agent or tour guide. This house also has to do with further advanced learning, so they might find themselves studying and aiming for a higher education. Sagittarius symbolizes the search for wisdom; this is the sign of the philosopher.

December is ruled by Sagittarius, and you can use this energy to learn to entertain people, whether you are a Sagittarius or not. When you entertain, you laugh and become part of it all. Things don't seem so serious when you are being entertained. Some of the great filmmakers have done more for people's spiritual developments than anyone else ever has. They entertain them, they tell stories and are willing to let people have their fantasies.

CAPRICORN

Capricorn is an earth sign and its ruling planet is Saturn. The key word for this sign is *'I Use'*. It rules the tenth house, which governs ones career, profession, leadership position and the relationship one has to the world. This is the most elevated point in the horoscope. Most Capricorns are ambitious and many plan their lives to follow a purposeful destiny. The energy of this sign gives Capricorns determination, perseverance, and great powers of endurance to reach their goals. They set high standards for themselves and expect the same from others. They have a great talent for management, and know how to organize and run the administration of a business. Because of their ability to have a clear vision of the goals they want to achieve, they are able to manifest whatever they set their mind to. Capricorns are considered conscientious, responsible, and hard working people, and they will refuse to acknowledge defeat. They have a tendency to be cautious and conservative, but just as you think they are being too serious, they may surprise you with a subtle, but witty remark that makes you laugh.

Capricorns have enormous admiration for people who work hard and attain success in reaching their goals. It inspires them to keep striving for their own goals. They are one of the most stable signs of the zodiac and are sure to end up on top of the ladder sooner or later. This sign symbolizes the goat climbing to the top of the mountain, and that is exactly what Capricorns aim for. The Capricorn energy has strong leadership qualities, and when they've reached their goals and have mastered the top positions in their field, they will turn around and help the people behind them so they, too, can reach their goals.

How is the emotional and romantic side of life for Capricorns? It may be suppressed by their practical common sense. To remain in balance, they need to learn how to relax and enjoy some fun once in a while or they will end up as much too serious and addicted to work. Their main assets are prudence, maturity, dedication, persistence, and thoroughness. Their faults are a general lack of sentiment and apprehension.

Capricorn rules January and this is a perfect month for anyone who wants to improve some of their Capricorn skills, such as setting some goals for yourself and be prepared to work steadily to reach them. You can use the Capricorn energy whether you are a Capricorn or not. Work hard to get organized for the holiday season, and then when it arrives, you can enjoy yourself and let go of the serious side of you.

AQUARIUS

Aquarius is an air sign and its ruling planet is Uranus. The key word for this sign is *'I Know.'* It rules the eleventh house of the horoscope and governs hopes and wishes. An Aquarius is the kind of person who will follow a dream. The Aquarian energy is unique. It is one of the most mysterious signs of the zodiac. In many ways it is considered the sign of the future. There are times when Aquarians feel at odds with other people unless they are of the same sign. It is not easy for people from other signs to understand the Aquarian mindset and what motivates them. They have a detached and elusive quality about them, which other people find hard to figure out. Aquarians are unorthodox and original people who don't want to follow the crowd and are therefore known as the different drummer.

Aquarians are seekers of knowledge and get excited when they discover new things to learn. They never get bored. They are outgoing, kind, friendly, and very people orientated and possess a great desire to help and serve others. Their love for all humanity is boundless. The love they feel for others is more on a universal level than a personal one. They are the humanitarians of the zodiac and concerned with the welfare of all the people on the planet. Aquarians enjoy being involved with groups or organizations for social causes where they meet, friends and connect with many new acquaintances. Aquarians are among some of the kindest people in the world, easy going, honest, and never mean-hearted. Many highly-evolved people are born under this sign.

Aquarius likes to feel free and independent and will sacrifice other things in order to maintain this independence. They are fixed in their opinions and can be unpredictable when people or situations are in disagreement with their ideas. They persist with their point of view when they settle on an idea they have carefully worked out. But then their ruling planet, unpredictable and impulsive Uranus, can suddenly create an unexpected change to everybody's surprise. Someone is in disagreement with their ideas and challenges their stubbornness, and Aquarius is able to let it go and cheerily seek a new path or plan to pursue.

Unconventional Aquarius is often ahead of everyone in their way of thinking. They welcome new and original ideas with excitement. They are unusually gifted individuals, intellectually clever, with good memories, and they are often among the world's leading and abstract thinkers –philosophers and scientists. They have a special kind of intuition, it's like an invisible electric wave they use to tune into other people's thinking.

The month of February is ruled by Aquarius and this is group energy. You can use this energy whether you are an Aquarius or not. The lesson to learn here is to be an individual in a group. It is how to remain true to your own identity and not to be influenced by others. We all have some qualities that will benefit others in the group and if everyone expresses their virtues, then they can be a role model to someone in the group.

PISCES

Pisces is a water sign and ruled by Neptune, the planet of mystery and illusion. Their key word is *'I Believe.'* It is the ruler of the twelfth house of the horoscope, the last sign of the circle, which governs institutions, hospitals and work you do behind the scene. Such as an author, scientist and designer. Pisces love to help people and are often found in hospitals as doctors and nurses.

Down through time, many people who studied astrology claimed Pisces was the most advanced energy of the zodiac. It is believed people who are born under this sign are old souls. Pisces governs reincarnation, eternity and spiritual rebirth. It is endowed with a brilliant sense of intuition, and, in fact, Pisceans tend to pick up the worries and troubles of others. They have the ability to sense other people's pain and are sympathetic toward them, and a Pisces will always be willing to lend a shoulder for someone to cry on, but because of their sensitive nature are often moved to tears too. Pisces are loyal, unselfish, and generous, and always ready to help a friend in need. However, there are times when they need their own space, because they take everyone's problems on-board, and are inclined to give away their strength that they need for their own emotional protection.

Pisces has a wonderful creative imagination. They can usually see beyond the imperfection and notice the beauty of the situation. If you have a Pisces as a friends, they will point out the teaching moment, so you can understand why you had to go through a certain situation. They inspire people to move on and reach for their highest potential so they can reach their goal.

Pisces are capable of great sacrifice and hard work in service to humanity. On the other hand, they are probably best suited for creative endeavors, because they are artistically inclined. Exposure to music and dance stimulates their originality. Pisces's ability to create fantasy can often produce some wonderful gifts for the world to enjoy. They can go into meditation and come out with ideas like no one else, and all Pisceans share in that gift.

The Pisces energy is about completion. This sign rules the month of March, and that is a good time to do a spring cleaning. You can use this energy whether you are a Pisces or not. Take a look at what you don't need any more in all areas of your life. This should be done on a physical, emotional, and mental level to give it completion. Say to yourself: *I am finished with this. It doesn't work for me any more.* It's not good to hang on to old things or people when your energy is vibrating at a different frequency. That will only drain you. You want to make room for the wonderful new energy that will come when you let go of the old worn-out things. It is so much better when you do it consciously, because when you have completed the old frequency without recognizing it, the universe does the completion for us, and then we usually see it as a failure.

Your Special Mission - Here In Life According To Your Sun Sign

Each one of the Sun Signs has a special mission here in life. Their ruling planet contributes to the unique and individual gift people born under one of the twelve signs was given at birth to fulfil their mission.

If everyone would use their talents or were able to follow their special mission, the world would probably be a much better place. Many people have not developed enough to realize they have certain gifts that they need to develop for them to become successful. Your life would be so different if you lived up to your full potential and used your talents for the good of everyone. When you do that, you open the door for many good things to come into your life.

What is your special mission?

Those of us in each of the Sun Signs who are fortunate enough to instinctively know what their special mission in life is, or maybe those who just have a feeling of the path they should follow, are the ones who turn out to be successful in adding value to the world and also to themselves.

There are lots of people who do not start out knowing their talent or special gifts. So, therefore, they work through many different stages developing certain aspects of themselves. Along their journey they discover new talents, not realizing they had those qualities all along.

Everyone makes mistakes and knows the feeling of being disappointed in themselves. But if we choose to look at these mistakes as learning experiences we have along the way to full realization of ourselves, it doesn't seem so bad. Learning through your own mistakes is the greatest teacher.

Design Your Destiny

Each Sun Sign bestows a special talent or gift to each person born under that sign. To help you get as much out of your talents as possible and design your own destiny, I have written the most likely talents for each of the twelve Sun Sign to give you and idea of what your special mission in life may be. It is always good to read about other successful people who lived up to their special mission, you can learn from them and think of them as your role model. Therefore, as an example of what can be achieved I have included famous people under each Sun Sign.

Aries And Your Special Mission

How are you going to achieve your special mission in life? When you were born under this sign you were given the gifts of courage and lots of dynamic energy to help you take action whenever needed. You have a good, clear mind that is able to see through other people's tricks and dishonesty and get straight to the point of the problem. These are the attributes that will help you get on your right path to fulfil your mission in life. People will know where they stand with you and sense you do believe in what you say to them and you will walk your talk.

The less evolved, daring and risk-taking Aries will always go for what he/she wants and with the intention of getting it whether it is for the good of everyone or not as long as his/her desire has been fulfilled. Many of these unevolved young Arians are using their energy in the wrong way and as children are guilty of harassing and making other's lives a misery. They will use unethical tricks when competing against one another and cause breakups between friends and create unhappiness for people around them, and, sooner or later for themselves.

However, if you are one of the more evolved Aries, then you will probably want to live up to your highest potentials and follow the call of your mission here in life. You have a limitless ability to serve humanity with your inspirational ways of encouraging and motivating others to reach their full potential. You walk forward and take the lead and show others who think their situation is hopeless by showing them that giving up is not an option. You motivate them not just with words, but you demonstrate with your actions and refusal to give up, which will inspire others and give them strength to carry on.

So what exactly is your mission? Aries are leaders, and you need to use all your courage and drive for a worthy cause much larger than just for yourself , but for the benefit of everyone. The more you stretch and challenge yourself, the closer you will become who you are meant to be. Helping the world to improve and become a better place is your mission. Once you decide to accept your ability to be a leader, you will be able to inspire people inspiring and lead others to accomplish their goal.

Many of the famous and successful people in the world who were born under the Sun Sign of Aries have already accepted their special mission and walked forward as role models for everybody to see. People who have not yet reached their full potential and find it hard to move forward should use these successful people as mentors for their own benefit, so they, too, can discover their special mission and work towards it.

Famous Aries and Their Mission Statement

Some famous Aries who succeeded in following their special mission are Kate Hudson- actress. Mariah Carey is well known for her wonderful singing voice, as well as her acting abilities. Sarah Jessica Parker – from Sex And The City. Sarah Michelle Gellar – star of Buffy the Vampire Slayer, and who has also branched into movies, like Scooby Doo. Jessica Lange – US actress.

Doris Day – actress and comedienne, of the 50s and 60s. Marlon Brando – actor born in 1924, star of many movies over the years. Claire Danes – American actress most famous for her role opposite Leonardo DiCaprio in 'Romeo And Juliet'. Chuck Norris and actor, Christopher Walken. These movie stars and great entertainers have made us laugh and cry and helped us to get in touch with our feelings.

Taurus And Your Special Mission

Taurus what is your special mission in life and how are you going to achieve it? Your love of the simple life and belief that a decent, hard working person can still get ahead here in life is what you demonstrate to the world. Many Taurus people planned their life down to a fine art that is uncomplicated and cater only for a simple and trouble-free lifestyle.

Most people born under the Sun Sign of Taurus are fairly easy going and good natured people. They are often misjudged by others for being an easy push over and for the most they are mistaken. You should never underestimate a Taurean. If you think you can take advantage of his/her easy going nature, think again. Once they have made up their mind, there is no one who can change it.

When you see your hard work paying off, your confidence in yourself will rise to new heights and strengthen your faith and your beliefs in hard work. It will help you be committed to finding your special mission in life.

The less evolved Taurean will in some cases suffer from a closed mind and be incapable of opening up to new ideas. Friends and families have a hard time convincing them that some changes are good.
However, when the more enlightened Taurus shows everyone they know how to stand their ground for the good of everyone, then they help to create hope for the average person.
In our changeable world, which is full of dishonest and insecure people, there is a great need for trustworthy people like Taurus. Their practical, common sense will win over the more screwed up and calculating people. Other people will sense their down to earth, calm manner and will place their trust in them, also enjoying their dry sense of humor.

Taurus is the solid rock everyone will lean on when times are difficult and problems seem overwhelming. The presence of their placid nature is enough to calm everyone. Taurus does not panic easily, because they know things usually always work out as they were meant to and we just need to have enough faith that, even though we have no control over the future, there is a higher power with a plan.
People will admire Taurus for being a person they can count on, one who will stick to their word and will not give up easily and run away from a complicated situation. Your special mission here in life is to show people that a Taurus can get ahead by being a good, honest, and hard working person just by using their practical down to earth attitude.

Famous Taureans and Their Mission Statement

The brilliant actor Jack Nicholson started off with small guest spots, but true to his sign as a Taurus, he kept sticking to what he felt was his mission, and he has given the world many enjoyable hours through his numerous movies. The handsome George Clooney started off as an actor getting a small part in a movie and was later offered bigger parts and became successful in the film industry by following his passion. Shirley Mclaine felt drawn to the world of show business. She had a natural talent for acting and entertaining an audience and she has done well to follow her calling, as she is an excellent actress. Other successful, famous Taurus celebrities include the soccer player David Beckham, the actress and singer Cher, and the singer, actress, and film director, Barbra Streisand. These are all people who have entertained ,and excited us by making us laugh and cry.

Gemini And Your Special Mission

Gemini, are you going to pursue your special mission? Your sign is the one of the twins, meaning there are two sides to your nature. It is natural for you to have these two sides come out now and again. One appears to be the good guy, and the other side is the bad guy. No other Sun Sign has the ability to change personality as quickly as the undeveloped Gemini twin. It is almost as if they have a voice inside them giving them contradictory advice, and they are not sure which side to follow.

In case you made up your mind not to undertake your special mission here in life, then you will probably float through life and take the easy way out and never experience the satisfaction you get from achieving your goal. The trouble is, you will continue to be in the same state of consciousness and never develop to your full potential. You may think you are on a good run and use your quick wit to charm your way out of adverse situations or simply disappear from the scene.

The Gemini who is not interested in following their special mission, but just wants to take the simple and uncomplicated way through life, may be inclined to screw other people and con them into investing their hard earned money in shaky deals. They might never be able to commit to one marriage, but will probably go through several relationships. But that is the unevolved Gemini. The ones who acknowledge and understand their special mission will apply their mental capacity and the command they have over the spoken word to express what others feel inside and therefore inspire and motivate them.

There are not many people who can encourage and shape minds in a positive direction like you can. You are able to use your brilliant mind to solve difficult and seemingly impossible missions, and transform problems into positive situations, because you have the clarity and logic to see little loopholes that other people miss. If you should have any disagreement with others, then you are usually the one who comes out as the winner because of the clever way you have with words. You can use your skill to support other people in complicated circumstances.

However, a less evolved Gemini can mature and turn their brilliant mind around and use it in a more positive way for the benefit of everyone. There may come a time when your logical mind can see how it can help you to use your talented mind in a constructive way. You may decide to design your destiny in a different way and go beyond yourself and look at the bigger picture. Because there are two sides to your personality you would make a good actor, a great debater or public speaker.

Famous Geminis and Their Mission Statement

The late President of United States John F. Kennedy was a Gemini. In his later teens he began to show an interest in politics and made it his mission and later became an immensely popular leader. Clint Eastwood started up as a young cowboy in the wild western movies and has made it his mission to act and engage people in a good story line for his films. The beautiful, late actress Marilyn Monroe struggled to make a name for herself in the movie industry and had many ups and downs during her career. She never gave up and kept following her passion until she became a household name. Other famous Gemini's who made their marks in the world are Judy Garland, Angelina Jolie, Kylie Minouge, and Nicole Kidman.

Cancer And Your Special Mission

Cancer, without a special mission you will wallow in your emotions and will only manage to think of yourself and your own needs. You'll feel there is a lack of love in your life and become needy and feel trapped in your own distress. You'll hardly think other people have needs, but are there for your benefit.

But that is the unevolved Cancer who has big dreams and desires, and when they are not met, react to those emotional feelings. After growing through much pain and mistakes, however, Cancers can learn from their experiences. When you grow into the more evolved and mature Cancer, you can turn those negative emotions around and use them in an unselfish way, and as a result, you will be transformed.

You will no longer have to figure out your own feelings, but can focus all your energy on more important issues other people have. When you help other people understand their emotions, you will replace your own hurt feelings with a sense of caring for others. Your mission in life is to nurture and care for others. Caner, you are the natural parent who comforts and guides people along. When they are in trouble, you are there for them. You will hug them and help them get over their pain.

Even though you love your home and family, you might be the type of Cancer who enjoys a career. If that is the case, then you will most likely turn your workplace into a second home and care about your co-workers as if they were your family. You will be the one who takes the new beginners and less fortunate under your wings and help them along until they can cope with the different tasks by themselves.

Caner, you are the mother of the zodiac and people sense your natural instinct for parenting and feel you are someone they can confide in when they need advice. The gift you bring to the world is to care and nurture the least capable people. That is, your mission in life.

Famous Cancers and Their Mission Statement

Some of the most famous people and celebrities born under the star sign Cancer are Princess Diana, The Dalai Lama and Nelson Mandela; these three people are a great example of how they follow their mission statement by caring for other people both in the physical and spiritual world. The following are famous actors who also put their mark on the world, Tom Cruise, Meryl Streep, Pamela Anderson, Sylvester Stallone, Tom Hanks and Robin Williams.

Leo And Your Special Mission

Leo your special mission is something you ought to start to develop at an early age before you start to follow your ego rather than your spirit. An undeveloped immature Leo can be so caught up in their ego that they will always want to be the center of everyone's attention. This sign is ruled by the sun, which is also the center of our solar system in our part of the universe.

If you always act as if you want to be the center of attention and the most important and special person there is and other people are only there to please you, then they will get tired of you. Of course you are important and special, but so is everyone else.

This may be a hard lesson for you, Leo, to discover, but the sooner you learn that, the sooner you will become aware of your mission and begin to write your mission statement and manifest your destiny. Just like everyone else, you have been given a gift, but not to use in a selfish manner. It is for you to share as a service for the benefit of others.

Leo you are one of the most gifted, talented, creative, and artistic people of the whole zodiac. Through the development of these gifts, you can teach others and lead them in the direction best suited for them.

Your special mission is to become a good leader and inspire everyone with your actions, because you will act as a role model for everyone to follow. You will not expect anyone to do something you haven't already done yourself.

So, Leo, if you choose to accept your mission in life, there is going to be a lot of hard work involved, and it is not always going to be easy. But in time, when you have achieved your goal, you will get the recognition. You will gain respect from others who will admire you for your achievement, and that will be incredibly rewarding for you, because it is something you have accomplished by yourself, and no one can take it away from you.

You will have the attention from everyone you so dearly love, but the difference is, now it is something earned through your hard work by following your special mission and not your ego.

Famous Leos and Their Mission Statement

President Barack Obama has followed his mission and become very popular with the people of the USA. Arnold Schwarzenegger worked hard and enthusiastically to gain respect through his many successful movies and his political and business career. Madonna pushed her way up the ladder as a pop singer and has gained recognition for her talent and much admiration for her ability to constantly change her image. The beautiful and sexy entertainer, Jennifer Lopez, has also managed to expand her career. Coming from nowhere, she, through her own effort, made a name for herself as a singer and achieved fame by following her calling.

Virgo And Your Special Mission

Virgo your special mission is not going to be hard for you to figure out, because it is so much part of your nature to be of service to humanity in whatever way you can. But if you are an unevolved Virgo, you are likely to make mistakes in the way you give service to others, and it might come across in the wrong way.

That could be because of your tendency to criticize others when they are doing their best. You do not mean to be critical, but you are almost fanatically concerned about details that you forget to encourage people for their work. Therefore, they lose interest and turn to something else.

Many people are careless about details and rush through life. When people skip the finer details in life they miss out on so much. They do not experience the depth of things and the satisfaction from having a job well done. But Virgo, you have been given this fine gift of an eye for details.

Now you just need to use it in a positive way, because even though your intentions are meant well, and you may be correct in your criticism, people will get discouraged if all you do is to criticize what they do. If they have been helping you with your project, they may decide to stop helping you and you will be left all alone.

However, if you choose to become aware that it is your special mission to give service to others through teaching your craft, then you have to stop being so critical and be more considerate of other people's feelings and learn to praise and inspire them to do better without any criticism. Then people will listen to you and realize you give them good, solid advice. They will respect you as a teacher and will be more than willing to help you with whatever project you are working on and be happy to learn more about the details that are so important.

There are many highly evolved Virgos who are following their special mission by giving service to humanity in a humble and modest way, yet with a strength of character appreciated by others.

Famous Virgos and Their Mission Statement

One of the famous people born under the Sun Sign Virgo, who has made her mark in the world through service to others is, first of all, Mother Teresa, who unselfishly devoted her life to helping people in need. Other famous Virgos are Michael Jackson, also is called the king of pop. He was one of the most significant entertainers of all time. His special mission was to entertain and bring joy and happiness to people. His songs and music still lingers on for people to enjoy, years after his passing.

Then there is the well-known American actor Adam Sandler, who gives his service through his many talents as a comedian, musician, screenwriter, and film producer. Famed actress Cameron Diaz has also followed her special mission for the benefit of the world.

Libra And Your Special Mission

Libra, you can live up to your special mission here in life if you tap into the latent talent you have as a leader. Libra has been described as having an iron fist in a velvet glove, and you set pretty high standards for yourself. You will charm your way through a disagreement and win, but allow the opponent to think they are the winners.

Libra is a cardinal air sign. However, you are usually not a self starter even though you are born under a cardinal sign, which gives you the intelligence to lead and take the initiative. However, you prefer to work with a partner who can take over the action while you give the advice and inspiration. You bring out the finest in people and kindly support those who lack the courage to follow their dreams.

These are the qualities of the evolved Librans, but what if you have trouble keeping your scales balanced? You like harmony and a peaceful life so much that you try to see the good in every situation and in people whether they deserve it or not. You will be optimistic and hopeful in the most awful circumstances and try to convince others things will be alright. That may work for a while, but deep inside you do not feel you are living up to what you know as being good and fair.

Libra is the sign of the diplomat, giving you the ability to be a mediator, someone who will bring the best out in people. Consequently, you tend to believe in everything that is good here in life. Your special mission is to bring peace, harmony, and a pleasant atmosphere into your surroundings, and also to create harmony between people. But as a Libra, you need to put up some boundaries and fight to protect your lifestyle, because there will always be people who have made a mess of their life, and try to move in and take advantage of the security you have so lovingly built up.

Libra, you have to become master of your destiny, which you can do by tapping into your own power and stick to it. Be willing to make the changes needed to carry out your special mission, even if it means letting go of a peaceful lifestyle for a while. The satisfaction and reward you will get from writing your own special mission statement and living up to it will more than give you the peace and harmony you so dearly crave.

Famous Librans and Their Mission Statement

Some of the famous people who have decided to work for the good of mankind as their mission statement were people like Eleanor Roosevelt and Mahatma Gandhi. The popular Margaret Thatcher, who was Prime Minister, of the United Kingdom from 1979 to 1990 made a huge contribution to the world by following her calling. In the later years we have seen famous people like Christopher Reeve, who, in his disabled situation, was able to inspire others. Linda McCartney, through her struggle with breast cancer was a Libran who lived up to her mission statement.

Scorpio And Your Special Mission

Scorpio, your special mission, whether you decide to accept it or not will have a powerful influence on your life. The traits of your sign, endow you with an intense, passionate, and strong nature, and when used in a positive way, will be enable you to help change people's lives, as well as your own, for your highest good.

The undeveloped Scorpio who has no idea what their special mission is unfortunately does not handle these strong traits so well. They feel the intensity of their nature and struggle to come to terms with these powerful traits. Controlling their emotion is a real challenge at times, and when they find themselves in difficult situations they get on the defense and verbally attack their opponent.

They can cause a lot of harm to other people, particularly to those who want to break away from their Scorpio friend because they find it hard to be around this strong, possessive energy. That is when the sting of the Scorpio comes out and their jealousy takes over. In these situations they can do some hurtful damage to others, but mostly to themselves.

You may be aware of the gifts of great power you were given at birth, and how powerful this influence is in your life. If you accept the challenge to make it your special mission to help other people, but after a while you might discover this powerful energy is too hard to handle. In that case, you may need some guidance in ways to develop your skill. There are many self-development courses around that can be of great help to you.

But if you use your gifts selfishly and for self gain just to satisfy yourself rather than helping other people, then it will not benefit you as much. If you decide to follow your calling and use your natural talents and gifts for the good of humanity so everyone can benefit from them, then you will gain tremendous rewards.

You will be given the respect and approval of others, which will fulfill the hungry cravings for success your intense nature longs for. The more evolved Scorpio is aware that the gifts he or she has been given is to share and use for a higher purpose, rather than keeping it selflessly for oneself. They know how to manage their destiny and make it their special mission to be of service to the world.

Famous Scorpios and Their Mission Statement

There are many famous Scorpios who have made a successful career out of their talents, and were able to share it. Bill Gates, the creator of Microsoft, helped millions and made him one of the richest men in the world. People use his creation of Microsoft every day. The famous actress Julia Roberts a Hollywood icon, who has made many hugely successful movies like *Pretty Woman* and *Erin Brockovich*. Demi Moore, an American actress, entertained her fans in movies like *G I Jane* and *Striptease*. The actress Jodi Foster started her career in Hollywood as a teenager. These are just a few of many successful Scorpios who wrote their special mission statement and stuck to it.

Sagittarius And Your Special Mission

Sagittarius, your special mission is first of all to tame your wild side, because it will say and do things that can easily get you into trouble. You are a very honest person, but sometimes you are too frank for your own good. You possess an excessive amount of energy, and there is also a side to you that enjoy the freedom that comes with independence. But without thinking and taking responsibility for your actions, you could create problems for yourself and others.

This wild side of yours needs to be controlled, or you can become accident prone. But let us assume you are able to control the wild side of you and let your higher self take over. Then it could lead you in the direction of your special mission. If you blend your physical energy with your higher intelligence and use it in a responsible way, then you, as well as other people, will benefit from it.

Sagittarius, you have so much to offer humanity, because your sign rules so many great and magnificent areas of life. These are in the vicinity of higher learning, travel, and long distance places, foreign languages, law, museums, books, and politics. You can take any one of these areas and apply them in a well-organized manner and turn it into your mission statement and make huge changes in your own life, as well as the world around you.

Many gifted and brilliant Sagittarians have accepted their special mission and become masters of their mind. They've designed their own destiny and achieved success. They've learned to use their intelligence and channel their energy in a disciplined way to develop their talents for the good of everyone, rather than use their gifts selfishly. Instead of being reckless with their energy, they've used wisdom and determination to accomplish whatever they set out to do. They are now able to teach their skillfulness to others. This results in admiration and respect and that Sagittarius should be your special mission.

Famous Sagittarians and Their Mission Statement

Among some of the famous Sagittarians who are excellent communicators and have lived up to their special mission statement through their careers is the successful super-model Tyra Banks, who, with her striking looks became an international sensation. She later helped young models to succeed in the modelling industry. The actress Judi Dench has entertained us with some wonderful movies. The talented singer Tina Turner overcame much adversity through an abusive husband and made a success of her career on her own. Frank Sinatra was a successful singer before he became an award-winning actor. This is just a few of many well-known Sagittarians who decided to follow through on their special mission statement.

Capricorn And Your Special Mission

Capricorn, having a special mission in your life is nothing new to you, because it is so much part of your nature to be ambitious and set yourself a goal. You would almost certainly feel motivated in your quest for progressing and climbing the ladder towards success.

You would find writing your own mission statement easy because you already know you want to accomplish what you set out to do. You would want to become financially well off through your own effort and hard work. Having all the good things you want in life and being able to cater to your own needs by being financially independent or at least close to it, is a worthwhile goal.

However, in your pursuit to follow your ambitions you need to acknowledge the spiritual side of your life, or you may end up with your goal, but no one to love. Because you were so focused on reaching your target, so you forgot about your loved ones.

When you design your destiny and write your mission statement, it should include helping others. Do not be selfish about your goal-setting, but make sure it is going to be something that will also benefit everyone else. If it doesn't, then you should be prepared to let it go. Many Capricorns managed to become wealthy and live a life of material comfort, but one that is lacking in spiritual warmth and love, because they devoted their whole lives to their career, and didn't take the time to share it with someone.

Try not to live your life focused only on the material, but be willing to share your wisdom. When you reach the top of the ladder, be ready to go back down and pick up the ones behind you so you can advise them, and give them insights into how you got to the top. It should be your special mission, helping others and showing them the way so that they, too, can become successful and reach their goal.

Famous Capricorns and Their Mission Statement

In the past, many Capricorns have been involved in missions for the benefit of the world, rather than for themselves, and being admired and loved for their work and contribution to mankind. Albert Schweitzer helped people in distant places who desperately needed assistance.

Joan of Arc born, in 1412, was a famous Capricorn. She began hearing the voices of saints who had already passed away long before. She guided the French army to victory in a war against England.

The famous actor Jim Carrey, who played in many films and made us all laughs of his many funny characters, is a successful Capricorn. All of these people lived up to a mission statement higher than themselves.

Aquarius And Your Special Mission

Aquarius, your special mission is unusual, but extraordinary, in a bizarre way. You are nothing like your neighboring sign Capricorn. If anything, you are just the opposite in character. Uranus is your ruling planet, which can present you with some unpredictable events you did not count on.

However, if you thought more deeply about it, then you would remember that some of your thought patterns could have helped to create the erratic situations you sometimes get yourself into. You are a humanitarian by nature, and you would never want to keep the gifts you were given at birth for your own selfish benefit. Aquarius, you are one of the most generous signs of the twelve in the zodiac, and you are happy to share your gifts with many other people.

Your common sense may not be your strongest aspect . If you don't have another planetary combination indicating a practical streak in your nature, your big heart may run away with you. That could stop you from living up to your high ideals and all the wonderful things you dream of doing for other people in need.

So Aquarius, your special mission would be to learn to take care of the self first, and find a way to educate yourself in a career where you can incorporate the humanitarian side of your nature. This way you will be able to pay your bills, and provide for yourself, and the people close to you. That would be the most sensible and realistic way for you to go forward, and it will give you a chance to work out a plan on how you can manifest your dream of helping humanity.

Famous Aquarians and Their Mission Statement

Here are some of the well-known humanitarians who put their marks on the world. These Aquarians caught everyone's attention on their long and important journeys by following their mission statement. Abraham Lincoln was one of the most amazing humanitarians the world ever produced. Thomas Edison, another famous Aquarian, invented the electric globe, which has benefited us all and is now part of our daily life.

The humanitarian actor Paul Newman had a successful film career, but is also well known for his charity work. The food company he founded made millions of dollars, which has all been donated to charity.

And then there is the amazing Oprah Winfrey, who has helped countless people turn their lives around in a positive way. Through her talk show, she was able to invite many interesting people who assisted her in bringing a constructive message to the people who needed help. She became the lifeblood of many people who turned on the TV every day to watch her show.

These are all people who used their gifts and took practical approaches to follow their high ideals as humanitarians to help other people. They made a big change in the world through their own effort. Aquarius, when your intentions are pure and honest, and you go about things in a logical way, you will be rewarded in many ways as you embark upon your special mission here in life.

Pisces And Your Special Mission

Pisces, your special mission is a personal one similar to your neighbor, the astrological sign, Aquarius. You need to control your loving, caring, and kind heart. You must learn to give all your love to the people who have really earned it, and not to the wrong people. The trouble is, you find it hard to make clever and shrewd decisions, so people often take advantages of your gullible and trusting nature.

Some of you Pisces are likely to be too easy-going and are strongly influenced by your surroundings. You have a tendency to fall prey to phony friends who will use your soft attitude for their own selfish intentions.

Your compassionate nature draws people to you in the hope you can help them sort out their personal problems. You are not easily shocked, so people can tell you anything and you will sympathize with them and support them in their unhappiness. But because you are such an emotional person, you take on their troubles and find it hard to detach from them.

All though you have an unselfish outlook, and the world would surely benefit from more of your kind of people, for your own sake, you do need to learn how to care for yourself first. You must wise up and design your own destiny, think deeply about how you can better your circumstances, and figure out your mission in life. If you don't, you will just make more mistakes and get depressed because you always put others before yourself.

In a case like that you may take to drugs, gambling, and other related stimulants to help you forget and avoid reality. However, that is not the answer. It will only add to your problem and not solve anything in the long run.

All Pisces have an artistic streak in their character and many kinds of great artists are born under the astrological sign Pisces, and have been lucky enough to have someone to back them up and encourage them to make use of their talents. Pisces when you learn to take control of your heart and your feelings, you will be able to lift your emotional nature up to a higher level. Then you will be loyal to your friends or any quest you choose to follow. The people in your life will feel fortunate to be around you, and you will find it a lot easier to live up to your own special mission statement in life.

Famous Pisces and Their Mission Statement

Albert Einstein, a famous great scientist and Pisces, received much public attention for the influence he had on the 20th-century vision of physical reality.

Michelangelo, another Pisces, was one of the most famous and greatest artists in the western world. He created beautiful works of art, sculpture, and architecture, as a mark of his special mission in life. The beautiful actress

Elizabeth Taylor, who started her acting career as a child and continued her acting as an adult, made many films for which she received two Academy Awards. She was a much loved actress and brought much enjoyment to the public through her movies and later her philanthropic work. Living up to their mission in life created a life full of joy and fulfillment for these famous people.

The Twelve Signs and The Four Elements

In the early history of Astrology the old astrologers divided the twelve signs of the zodiac into groups of the four elements – fire, air, water and earth. The relationship between any two people depend to some degree on which of their ruling elements interrelate. The interpretation of the different combinations of signs and elements is explained in a general way. There is no perfect rule when these principles are applied to the abbreviated Sun Sign horoscope. However, it is important to know to which of the elements your Sun Sign belongs and how it affects your interactions with others.

Fire signs: Aries, Leo, Sagittarius. Air signs: Gemini, Libra, Aquarius. Water signs: Cancer, Scorpio, Pisces. Earth signs: Taurus, Virgo, Capricorn.

Fire Signs

Fire is compatible with fire and air, apart from the opposite pairs which you can find easily in a horoscope. These are Aries-Libra, Leo-Aquarius, and Sagittarius-Gemini. There can be a powerful first attraction between the opposite signs, but after a while, they each have to admit that they are not so compatible after all. Aries are quick to make decisions, but it can be hard for Libra to make a decision and the tension between them can cause friction. Leo is a fire sign, Aquarius is an air sign, but they are both fixed signs and have set opinions about their beliefs. Sagittarius a fire sign and Gemini an air sign. They can be attracted to each other, but also repel. Fire does not combine readily with water or with earth signs.

Air Signs

Air is compatible with air and fire. As mentioned above, Sagittarius – Gemini opposition can have some attractions for each other, but it may not work out well between them in the long run. The Libra-Aries attraction may not last too long when Aries needs action in their lives and Libras love to be surrounded by peace and harmony. Aquarius-Leo, may bring conflict when Aquarius acts out her unpredictable nature, which Leo finds hard to cope with. Air does not have much in common with Earth and Water.

Water Signs

Water is compatible with water and earth, but not in cases where the signs are on opposite sides of the zodiac chart. The Cancer-Capricorn opposition can cause conflict in a relationship if Capricorn becomes too ambitious and neglects sensitive Cancer. The Scorpio-Taurus opposition can certainly ignite a strong physical attraction, but they need more in common for a lasting bond. In case of the Pisces-Virgo opposition, how will practical Virgo cope with intuitive emotional Pisces? If they are willing, they could learn a bit from each other. Water has little affinity with fire or air, so they are danger zones.

Earth Signs

Earth is compatible with earth and water. As explained above, some conflict may develop with a water sign in opposition to an earth sign in the horoscope. A match up of Capricorn – Cancer opposition will have similar clashes to the other two sign combination, Taurus-Scorpio, Virgo-Pisces. The earth signs are practical while the sensitive water signs possess a very intuitive nature, which might be hard for the earth sign to cope with or understand. Earth does not mix easily with fire or air, either.

Combining The Zodiac Signs Compatibilities

Let us start with the first sign of the zodiac, Aries and discover the kind of chemistry this sign has with the rest of the Sun Signs. How well will their elements mix in different kinds of relationships, such as marriage, friendships, love affairs, and the family as well as a business partnership. All possible combinations of the twelve signs are listed below. The connection you may have with an acquaintance may not be so apparent, as it takes time to get to know another person better. However, this is only a general analysis of the compatibility between the Sun Signs. On a deeper level you would look for a Sun/Moon positive aspect. Like, does the Sun in John's horoscope form a positive aspect to the Moon in his girlfriend, Kate's, horoscope or vice versa? Or where is Venus placed in your chart? Is it in a favorable aspect to your partner's chart. These are details you would look at when you have your own personal horoscope drawn up and read to you by a professional astrologer.

Aries With Aries

This Fire Sign combination is compatible. Although it can be unpredictable, that is how they like it. Sex can happen anywhere or anytime, lots of excitement is what keeps their infatuation with each other ignited. Aries is a competitive sign, and if you both want to take the lead, it could result in disagreement and build up tension between you. This combination will not be a relaxed and peaceful one, but it will not be boring and could be rather exciting with a fun-filled atmosphere. If either one of you should get into any difficult situations, the other one would defend you with a fiery passion.

Aries With Taurus

Fire with earth is not the best combination. The characteristic of each sign is very different. Aries requires the stimulation of new enterprises or challenges. Aries will get impatient with the Taurean's need for security and wanting to stay in the same place. Aries is more action-oriented, but Taurus prefers stability in his/her life and needs to save and know they have financial security behind them, whereas Aries likes to spend and will happily venture into a new adventure and see where it takes them. Even though they are both highly sensual people, it is not going to be an easy match. Aries may be annoyed by the fixed pace and unimaginative lovemaking of Taurus. Aries love to have fun and be active and will be creative in ways that offers an outlet. If his project doesn't work out, however, he will appreciate the Taurus calmness and reliability. If Taurus will let Aries be the leader, then they may discover new sensual pleasure in each other.

Aries With Gemini

Fire with air is a pleasant combination, and because you both create a sparkling atmosphere, life will never be boring. Gemini's intelligence and wits are equal to Aries fighting spirit. Both of you enjoy variety, action, and discovering new things, so you will have many interests in common. Gemini's active and tireless mind inspires Aries to take notice and listen to the twins logical ideas. Aries inclination to control and take the lead is somehow restricted, because he is intrigued by the clever and versatile Gemini. Aries dynamic spirit and intelligent mind blends in well with Gemini's adaptability to change. In their love life, Aries is most likely to be the leader, and Gemini, is more than happy to contribute to the activity with new ideas. This union could lead to a successful marriage.

Aries With Cancer

Fire with water can create problems unless you search for common ground. When you just look at the two Sun Signs, then you would definitely say no, this combination is not going to work. Here we have home loving, sensitive Cancer, and fiery, frank, abrupt, but fun-loving adventures Aries who hates to be tied down. There is bound to be some emotional clashes and tension between them, which would probably cause conflict for them sooner or later. The initial sexual attraction may have been enjoyable at first, but eventually they have to face reality. They are two different personalities with very dissimilar interests. This union will experience many ups and downs, and unless there are other positive compatible connections in their charts, be prepared for a stormy relationship.

Aries With Leo

Fire with fire is usually a positive combination. These two signs are equally outgoing, extroverted, warm, and vibrant. This is two strong personalities with large egos, which may get in the way when the other person starts being bossy. No way will Aries take second place to Leo, the regal sign of the zodiac, who wants to be the center of attention. A few problems can arise when they both want to be the one in charge. They both possess a dynamic personality with lively desires. If they are willing to share the lead and Aries will allow Leo to be in the limelight now and again, which means a lot to Leo, then that would be a gesture of true commitment to each other. As lovers they are a perfect match, and being so much alike sexually could be the chief thing that makes them forget and forgive each other as their emotional needs are met.

Aries With Virgo

The Fire signs are volatile and impulsive, whereas earth signs tend to be practical, sensible, stable, and self controlled. In this combination Aries need to exercise a lot of patience, which might be hard for this sign. Reserved Virgo may be amazed by the outgoing nature of Aries. However, this duo's sexuality is very different, and they would have to give each other some time to appreciate each other's needs. Aries are direct, passionate, and spontaneous, while Virgo's sexuality is more mysterious, and it takes time to discover the needs of this person. Aries will naturally take the lead and excitingly plan new projects for them. Virgo will soon destroy the glow in Aries by criticizing and finding details that could go wrong. Their emotional nature is so different that there would need to be lots of other favorable aspects in their charts for these two people to come together in a happy relationship.

Aries With Libra

The Fire signs have a natural affinity with air signs. However, these two signs are opposite each other in the zodiac. At first, there is a strong physical or emotional attraction between them. They both take pleasure in their sexual interaction, but Libra likes to take things a bit slower and gentler, and might be put off by the fast pace of Aries. Instinctively, they sense that the other person's personality has qualities they are missing. Aries can be very demanding and aggressive. All this could be too much for Libra, and he/she might look for someone not quite so challenging. Aries will go on another adventure in search for a more suitable partner. This combination would never last for long and marriage between these two signs is doubtful.

Aries With Scorpio

Fire with water creates a highly-charged relationship. Mars is the ruler of Aries. In the past Mars was also considered the ruler of Scorpio until Pluto was discovered and made the ruling planet of Scorpio. They are two powerful planets and each sign will appreciate the strengths of the other person's abilities. Aries is open and straightforward, whereas Scorpio is secretive and a deep thinker, which could be difficult for Aries to understand. They are both fiery, independent, and do not like to be controlled. If any disagreement develops between them, it may spoil any chances of experiencing the extraordinary, passionate sex life they could enjoy and share with each other. If they can agree on aiming for the same goal, then they might have excellent teamwork.

Aries With Sagittarius

Fire does not conflict with fire. It could be quite a compatible combination. Mars is the ruler of Aries and Jupiter the ruling planet of Sagittarius. These are two very independent signs, and if they allow each other the much needed freedom they require, then they could be the perfect match for each other. Sagittarius will inspire Aries in his new ventures, who in turn will be thankful for the other sign's happy go lucky and optimistic attitude, as well as honesty. They both posses a good sense of humor, which will get them through issues that can occur along the way. The physical attraction in their love life promises to bring the twosome excitement in their relationship, and their sex life will not be boring. Both signs like a fast pace, so there will be little time for relaxation, but that is the way they like it. Neither one of them will tolerate the other person being bossy.

Aries With Capricorn

The combination of fire with earth can be stressful. They are two very dominating signs. Aries is ruled by the fiery planet Mars, which bestows him/her with an impulsive personality, someone who often jumps into things before having done any research, but will plan as they go along and hope for the best. Aries likes to act impulsively and hates having to wait. On the contrary, Capricorn like to plan a long time ahead and do a thorough research before cautiously starting something new. Capricorns are ruled by the planet Saturn, which gives them a very cautious and patient nature. Without wanting to, security minded Capricorn can squash Aries and strip this sign of their optimistic, adventurous attitude. On the other hand, Aries may be too overpowering with his enthusiasm, and shock Capricorn with his reckless spending. Capricorn will carefully save for a rainy day and along comes Aries and blow it all. That is going to cause some strong conflicts. Aries will find their love life too boring when Capricorn only prefers sex at a set time.

Aries With Aquarius

Fire is compatible with air. Mars, the ruler of Aries, and Uranus the ruler of Aquarius, is a powerful connection. If they love each other enough, the pair has the potential for a happy union. Both signs can be a bit unpredictable, that is a trait they will have to be prepared to accept in each other. Aquarius is the humanitarian of the zodiac. Aquarius will always want to encourage the enthusiastic spirit of Aries whenever he/she starts a new project. Aries also enjoys the unique energy of Aquarius, who are often inventors and can come up with some original ideas that might even lead to new discoveries. The prospect of starting something completely new is right down Aries's alley, who also has the ability to come up with new ideas, adding to the excitement of the probability of a new start. Sexually, this duo may not be as hot as Aries would like, but if he/she is being considerate of Aquarius emotions, then this couple should enjoy a happy relationship.

Aries With Pisces

Aries and Pisces, your ruling planets – fiery Mars and watery Neptune – are completely different in nature. These two signs are worlds apart. Aries is a positive and active sign, not afraid to give it a go even if the last venture was unsuccessful. Emotional Pisces on the other hand, can appear to be vague and indecisive. Pisces also possesses a strong intuition and has the ability to pick up on other people's feelings. This may appeal to Aries, who likes to dominate, so here is a challenge to conquer for Aries. When he/she discovers the unexpected, mysterious side of Pisces in the bedroom, he/she gets a delightful surprise. This will probably be where they bond and overcome any difference in their temperament and spend enjoyable times together. If they can make it as lovers, then the possibilities for marriage could be their next step. Most couples have had to work on their relationship for it to be successful. But if the right chemistry is there between two people, they have every chance for a happy union.

Taurus with Taurus

Bringing two earth signs together will definitely create a very stable couple. However, it may not be such an exciting union. They are both down to earth people and if they should embark out on some sort of adventure their cautious nature will make sure to plan well ahead. Their love life will probably not be to exhilarating, because their sex life will most likely lack the dynamic chemistry that drives a couple together. The Taurus man might be too earthy and the woman to emotional. They do have some things in common which is security and the love of money. They will no doubt both be hard working and strive for a secure lifestyle. Jealousy can be a problem if the woman doesn't feel she gets enough attention from her man. The best thing that would help this couple make their partnership work would be to get some interests outside of their relationship. Maybe develop some personal talents or spend more time with friends so their tendency to be possessive will ease off. That way they may bring more excitement into the relationship.

Taurus with Gemini

Taurus is an earthy sign and one of the most stable people of the zodiac. But to be matched up with changeable, restless, and airy Gemini could be very unsettling for Tausus, who likes things to remain the same. It will be a hopeless task trying to control and pin down vigorous Gemini. Some Taurus's are fascinated by the imagination and skillful ways Gemini handle change. However, Gemini has trouble accepting Taurus's slow reaction to his/her ideas. Taurus has a natural instinct to be possessive, but will find it very hard to hold on to Gemini, whose mood can be unpredictable, as there are two sides to this sign. The sex life between this duo doesn't look promising. It will be hard for Taurus to appreciate the different, changing moods of Gemini. One moment they act happy and playful, but then his/her sexual desires can change into a sizzling hottie. The mix of these two signs is not the best combination for a marriage unless there are other strong, compatible power points connecting in their horoscopes that will override the Sun signs.

Taurus with Cancer

The natural attraction with earth and water imply that you will get along well. Your mindset will be similar and you both need the security of knowing you have an affectionate and loving partner you can rely on. Your emotional nature is alike and you enjoy showing love and care for each other. Taurus enjoys the attention and protection Cancer takes pleasure in giving. You are both conservative and if any emotional conflict should arise between you, then you will most likely be able to talk it over. Taurus tends to rely on common sense and is capable of using logic to smooth things out when Cancer's changing mood come out. For these two signs to have a successful sex life, Taurus needs to understand that emotional Cancer wants a stable and loving relationship. This couple has the potential for a happy marriage if the two of you are willing to give of yourselves, rather than expect the other person to always give.

Taurus with Leo

Taurus and Leo are both two strong-willed fixed signs. They may need to learn to compromise if they are to get along well. It is natural for Taurus to be very affectionate. It is part of his/her nature and Leo, who enjoys attention, is loving it. Leo has a dominating personality and Taurus, who is patient, will tolerate this for a while, until one day he has had enough and the bull will show his horns. Leo is extravagant and like to spend, whereas Taurus is cautious when it comes to money. This could cause conflict between the two signs. However, there is a strong physical and emotional attraction between them, and both signs possess a magnetic sex appeal. If Taurus is willing to keep on adoring Leo, and he/she will return the emotional affection he/she needs, then perhaps it can work.

Taurus with Virgo

Two earth signs together signify you are on the same page. These are two practical, realistic, and very capable people who have a lot in common and share a similar desire for material success. But on the emotional side, you are very different. The two of you may fall in love easily, but when it comes to your sex life, Virgo likes things to be uncomplicated. Taurus doesn't mind that. However, Virgo, whose feelings are usually under control, can feel a bit uneasy when Taurus gets too emotional and acts in a possessive manner, trying to bring other methods into their love life to spice things up. Apart from that, there should not be many problems. This couple is a good mix. Virgo's razor sharp mind and Taurus's stability should make a good union. Both signs want security, and if they exercise patience with each other, there is every chance for a successful partnership.

Taurus with Libra

Earth sign Taurus and air sign Libra are from two very different elements, but even though there is little similarity amid these two signs, there is a strong bond. Venus is the ruler of their sign and therefore they share a love of art and music. They will enjoy being involved in the artistic world. They appreciate the beauty of the finer things in life, so there is not likely to be much conflict between this couple, because they both take pleasure in a peaceful and harmonious lifestyle. Taurus is stubborn, but Libra can carefully and in a tactful way manipulate Taurus around to soften his/her thoughts to Libra's way of thinking. Libra likes a bit of romance in his/her relationship and can easily turn on the charm. Taurus, however, might get jealous of his/her flirty antics. They are sexually compatible, so they could spend a lot of pleasurable times together.

Taurus with Scorpio

These two signs are compatible, even though they are opposite signs in the zodiac. Taurus is an earth sign and Scorpio is a water sign. Although they are from two different elements, they are well-matched. In a love relationship, it will bring an irresistible physical attraction. Because they both have a strong sexual craving they will make a good team. They are both stubborn and jealous by nature, and that can be a cause of conflict for them. The intense feelings between these two signs can resort to fury if pushed too far. This could result in a turbulent union. If they can build enough trust in their relationship, there is every possibility for a successful marriage.

Taurus with Sagittarius

Here we have two very different signs, Taurus, earth and Sagittarius, fire. Taurus is such a stable sign and likes to feel secure and has a strong need to possess its loved one. That doesn't go down too well with Sagittarius, who takes great pleasure in feeling free and independent. This fire sign likes to be active and enjoys changes, even if it is just changing around the furniture to give the room a different look. Sagittarius loves to travel and visit distant places. He/she needs plenty of room, both mentally and physically, whereas Taurus feels more secure staying put. However, although they are two different personalities, sexually Taurus will enjoy Sagittarius, but can also become fuming mad with his/her easygoing ways when it comes to sex. Taurus always tries to provide a good home, but unless there are other compatible planets in their horoscope, it is not going to be an easy mix. But true love can overcome many differences.

Taurus with Capricorn

Taurus and Capricorn are two earth signs, so this is a compatible combination. Security minded Taurus will always be thankful for Capricorn's sensible attitude and down-to-earth approach to life. Both signs have a good sense of the other person's character. They both like money and will make sure there is a good backup in the bank for future expenses. They are both very conservative and strive to make a secure life for themselves. Capricorn, who is ambitious, will be willing to work hard for the two of them. Patient Taurus will be eager to encourage Capricorn to persevere whenever it is required. Capricorn may appear to be reserved by nature, but under that front is a much softer person with a healthy sexual appetite. If sensual Taurus is prepared to make the effort to dig deep and tune into Capricorn's softer feelings, then there is every chance for a perfect union.

Taurus with Aquarius

These two earth and air signs don't have much in common. This is a mixture of two strong-minded signs who are basically very different in nature. Taurus is conservative with the major focus on his/her possessions. A Taurus will find it hard to understand the unpredictable behavior of Aquarius, who is the humanitarian of the zodiac, to the point of being distressed about the welfare of other people. Aquarius likes to feel free to share friendly affection with many different people. Taurus is possessive of his/her partner and will not be not at all happy about sharing their feelings with everyone. Aquarius's carefree outlook on love will confuse sensual Taurus, who has a need for the physical connection and wants to make love and not just talk about it. Aquarius doesn't put a lot of importance on sex. Taurus will not be happy with this attitude, which could cause conflict between them. This is not the best combination unless there are planets in their horoscopes suggesting otherwise.

Taurus with Pisces

The combination of these two signs, earth and water, is a good match because they are of a similar temperament. Their ruling planets, Venus and Neptune, are not at odds, but are very compatible. Taurus will act as a dependable partner who is determined to provide security and stability for wavering Pisces. Taurus is a practical realist in his/her way of thinking, while Pisces often has his/her head in the clouds and is ruled by emotions. But, down to earth Taurus has a way of bringing Pisces back to reality. The mixture of these two elements can be a good balance if each person is willing to learn from the other. They both have a love of art, and the one strong point they share is their appreciation for beauty, art, sensuality, and all the good things in life. They are both artistically minded, but especially Pisces, who probably dreams of accomplishing something special. Pisces may be able to help Taurus to use his/her imagination. There is a strong possibility that these two signs will make a happy union.

Gemini with Gemini

Two air signs together, Gemini with Gemini, both ruled by Mercury, is a fascinating combination. This will be an active couple with lots of friends and many interesting and stimulating conversations with people from all walks of life. They may be highly strung, but this excitable pair love to meet new people and are happy to join in wherever a social gathering is happening. They make a great team and others will enjoy their company. Sex is such fun for them, but although they are very much in harmony with each other sexually, they may get bored if they can't think up some sort of variety to spice things up. There will be a lot of love between them and marriage is sure to be in the cards. This will be one of the most fascinating couple among your friends.

Gemini with Cancer

Gemini is an air sign and its ruling planet is Mercury, and therefore, mentally oriented. Cancer is the water element and ruled by the Moon, which governs the emotions, so there is a noticeable difference in their natures. Variety is what spices up Gimini's life, and makes him/her excited, but this can be disturbing for Cancer, who loves to create a home for the family. Gemini is not a deep thinking sign, so Cancer's emotional moodiness will not affect Gemini too much. He/she is much too busy doing other things to worry about that. Cancer may feel neglected and put on a hurtful attitude to get his/her attention, but unfortunately it doesn't work with this kind of partner. At first Cancer was attracted to Gemini, but will in time find it hard to go along with his/her liberated sexual energy. Cancer is home loving, whereas Gemini is very sociable and would become restless to have to stay locked up at home all the time. Unless the other strong power points in their horoscopes are compatible, this union doesn't promise a long time connection.

Gemini with Leo

The element of these two signs is air and fire and they should be able to get along well, especially on a mental or intellectual level. Leo likes to be the center of attention, but Gemini has so many interests that he/she hasn't got time to pay attention to Leo all the time. Naturally, Leo will feel neglected and may try to dominate Gemini. That might overwhelm Gemini's free spirit and cause conflict. Socializing is something they have in common, but Gemini is flirtatious by nature, and this may hurt Leo's self-confidence. This could be a problem, but if they can get past that and enjoy all the good fun they do together, things should work out well for them. They both have passionate and emotional needs when it comes to their sex life. Warm hearted Leo enjoys Gemini's diverse desires. If each person will allow the other to be true to their own character, then this couple can be a sparkling union.

Gemini with Virgo

Mercury rules both Gemini and Virgo, which bestows them with a common mental point of view on most things. This can be inspiring in many areas of their lives. Both signs have their emotions under control when dealing with the mental side of their business. Virgo is usually level headed, and has a of matter-of-fact and no-nonsense attitude. He/she will not always appreciate Gemini's many ideas and impractical plans. However, Virgo can laugh it off because with Mercury as its ruling planet, this sign is endowed with a joyful, funny side and wins people over with its dry sense of humor. This duo may get along as good friends, but as lovers, they would not be a good match. Virgo's image of what their sex life should be like is not at all what changeable Gemini has in mind.

Gemini with Libra

These two air signs are compatible. Gemini is ruled by Mercury, the planet of the mind, and Libra's ruling planet is Venus, which represents beauty and the affection you need. Venus has a need to generate a harmonious atmosphere, where each person can be appreciated for their own unique qualities. This sign wants to connect with others whose personality complements their own. This couple will create a union, which has a mutual appreciation of all refined art. They both take pleasure in beautiful things and enjoy socializing with people. Gemini likes to communicate and participate in interesting conversation, so is more than happy to share ideas with Libra, who is pleased to have someone with whom they can also share their thoughts and feelings. Libra is highly sexed and very loving, and their lovemaking will never be boring. This is an ideal connection and they will make a happily married couple.

Gemini with Scorpio

The element of air and water will not be a trouble-free mix. These two signs are very different in their personalities. The intensity and magnetic power of Scorpio will inundate Gemini, who will feel squashed and run for his/her life to protect his/her free spirit if Scorpio gets too possessive. Gemini loves to socialize, where as Scorpio tends to be more of a private person. However, they could make a good team if they learn to get along together. Gemini has an amazing imagination and is full of good ideas. Scorpio knows just how to give some of those great ideas an appealing appearance to make them irristible to the buying public, so they would make a good business partnership. Scorpio is very sensual with a deep, strong passion for sexual togetherness, whereas restless Gemini is too lighthearted and is not so devoted. Unless there are other compatible power points in their horoscopes it is not going to work out as a happy marriage, but maybe as a business partnership.

Gemini with Sagittarius

Air with fire are two stimulating elements together and can be a good combination. As opposite signs in the horoscope, they can be attracted to each other, but they can also be appalled with one another. Both of them like to live busy lives and allow each other the freedom they enjoy so much. Their lives are filled with many interests, and they take a lot of pleasure in spending quiet moments together sharing their experiences. Gemini has a wonderful energy for love and can see beauty in almost anything. Sagittarius has a great sense of humor, and it is natural for him/her to have a good laugh. They are both lighthearted and easy going people and sexually this duo could be fun. Their downfall might be that neither of them shows any intense passion, and that is an area they should work on to make this union as ideal as possible.

Gemini with Capricorn

Easy going free-spirited air sign Gemini and serious earth sign Capricorn are two very different natures. However, if Gemini really wants to get along with the Saturn-ruled sign, he/she will find a way to communicate. Being one of the great communicators of the zodiac, and the ones who build the communication bridges between people, it should not be too difficult. Capricorn, who steadily works toward his/her goal until it is reached, is endowed with a lot of wisdom. Gemini is fascinated by this and keen to listen and learn. It might be hard for Capricorn to understand the lightheartedness and changeable nature of Gemini. But on the other hand, Capricorn can also be a non-stop talker, so by talking it over, they could communicate and be willing to learn from one another. If Gemini put on his/her flirtatious charm, Capricorn might find it refreshing to leave ambitions behind for a while and indulge in a sexual relationship with cheerful Gemini. Each sign can enrich each other with their unique gifts.

Gemini with Aquarius

These two air signs are compatible in lots of ways. Although their ruling planets, Mercury and Uranus, are functioning on different planes, the elements will pull them together. Changeable Gemini is not bothered by the detached nature of Aquarius, and finds his/her unpredictable moods a bit of a challenge. Gemini, who is interested in the artistic side of life, is fascinated by Aquarius's originality and inventiveness. They both love to socialize, and are often involved with many groups of diverse friends. This is an unconventional relationship with unpredictable situations, which will help to keep it exciting. Physically, Aquarius is attracted to Gemini, and the feeling is mutual. There will be an intense sexual attraction between them, and it could lead to a happy marriage.

Gemini with Pisces

There is a vast contrast between these two signs. Gemini is air and Pisces is of the water element. Their energy is vibrating at a different frequency and it will be difficult for them to adjust to each other. Gemini has a logical mind, and is realistic and mentally alert. Pisces has an emotional nature and will most likely be hurt by Gemini's lighthearted attitude. Many Pisces have artistic abilities and possess a vivid imagination and often appear dreamy. He/she is very impressionable, with a well developed intuition that tends to pick up other people's feelings. Even though these signs are of different elements, they are both very adaptable signs. They may not understand each other, but they will tolerate the other person's outlook on life and accept that their personalities are dissimilar. If they should happen to have a romantic affair, it will probably be short lived.

Cancer with Cancer

Cancer is ruled by the Moon. This is a very sensitive water sign. They are both emotional by nature, and although they will understand the other person well, they are too much alike to create a really happy and satisfying couple. Feelings and emotions will be the main aspect in their life. They both get easily hurt and take every criticism to heart. They will always be there for each other, though, when one of them has a problem. Together, they will try to work it out, but the trouble is that their emotions make it hard for them to think clearly under difficult circumstances. Physically, they are drawn to each other, and their relationship can be rather sensual. A marriage between these two people will require a lot of care and understanding for one another.

Cancer with Leo

Even though water and fire are not well-matched, your individual rulers, the Moon and the Sun, harmonize. In spite of their dissimilar personality, there will be a strong connection. Cancer may have to stand back and give into dominant Leo demands, especially when it comes to their sex life, but is happy to let Leo take the lead. When Cancer's mood changes, Leo knows just how to make Cancer snap out of it. Leo has the ability to make his/her Moon shine more cheerfully. Leo loves to be admired. He/she needs a lot of attention, which Cancer enjoys giving. This couple could have a happy and fulfilling marriage.

Cancer with Virgo

Water is compatible with earth. This pair has the right qualities needed for a successful relationship. Cancer, who is a genuine, loyal, and reliable person, will appreciate the part of Virgo that pays careful attention to details. Virgo is known as a perfectionist, and if they are not, then they are here on earth to learn that in this lifetime. Cancer is bestowed with a patient nature and is prepared to let Virgo do things in his/her own good time to get as close to perfection as possible. The downfall of their relationship may be if Virgo criticizes sensitive Cancer too much. This couple's chances for a happy union are very promising, providing Virgo will demonstrate his/her feelings a little more and show love and affection towards emotional Cancer.

Cancer with Libra

The element of water and air are usually not very compatible. But in this case, the ruler of Cancer and Libra, the Moon and Venus, complement each other and are in harmony. Venus is the planet of love and beauty. This wonderful energy of Venus influences the way they express their feelings. The Moon governs the emotions, feelings, compassion, and affection. Cancer is very sensitive and his/her feelings are easily wounded. Peace-loving Libra will do just about anything to avoid conflict, and if he/she is not strongly aggravated, he/she will not cause any argument on purpose. Libra will welcome Cancer's natural instinct to give love and protect their loved one. However, Libra can sometimes feel a bit overwhelmed by Cancer's emotional nature. Libra needs some intellectual stimulation in their communication to balance all the emotional interaction. Libra also likes a bit of glamour, luxury, and romance to spice up their love life to keep the flame burning. Cancer will need to become aware of Libras cravings, if he/she wants the relationship to remain warm and exciting.

Cancer with Scorpio

The two water element signs, Cancer and Scorpio, are compatible and well suited for each other. Each one of the signs is intuitive and sense what is going on with the other person, so mutual trust is important to both of them. Sensitive Cancer has a high regard for the power and strength of Scorpio and appreciates the feeling of being protected. Scorpio can be very possessive and jealous of his/her love interest, but there will not be any reason to worry with this water sign, because Cancer will be faithful and emotionally committed to the relationship. Scorpio is a passionate lover, while Cancer is more inhibited about sexual desires, but wants to please her partner. Scorpio feels safe knowing Cancer is emotionally dedicated to him/her. This union should make a good, loving marriage that will only grow stronger with time.

Cancer with Sagittarius

Water with fire is not a good combination if there is no other compatible planetary influence in other important areas of the horoscope. In this mixture we find a lot of difference in their characters. Sagittarius has a free and happy-go-lucky nature, and this can make sensitive Cancer feel insecure. Water destroys fire, and that might be what he/she unintentionally will do, because Cancer needs a partner he/she can trust who will be protective. These two signs will need to work on learning to communicate to get a better understanding of each other. It is going to be hard to pin free-loving Sagittarius down to be the faithful, protective partner that Cancer so desperately wants. Cancer tends to be clinging, which can make Sagittarius feel repressed or trapped. He/she is an active lover and Cancer is easily pleased. There may not be enough adventure in their love life to keep Sagittarius happy.

Cancer with Capricorn

Cancer is a water sign and Capricorn is an earth sign, as a rule these two elements are very compatible, but they are in opposition to each other in the horoscope. Capricorn tends to be ambitious and aims for a successful goal. That attitude is not going to go down too well with Cancer, who feels hurt and neglected, because Capricorn is too busy paying attention to his/her career. Capricorn has a sense of duty and responsibility to provide well for his/her partner and family. Cancer respects that, but only wishes he/she would show more warmth, love, and affection toward him/her. Cancer is ruled by the Moon, which gives him/her an amazing imagination, as well as a brilliant memory. If Cancer learned to direct his/her attention on developing the amazing artistic talent he/she has, then he/she might be more fulfilled and not feel so neglected. Capricorn's ruling planet is Saturn, which bestows him/her with a serious outlook on life, but should be admired for his/her determination to work hard to become successful. A marriage between these two signs would only occur if both partners were prepared to fulfill each others demands.

Cancer with Aquarius

Cancer is a water sign and ruled by the Moon. Aquarius is an air sign and its ruling planet is Uranus. The only thing they would have in common would be that both signs are humanitarian and care a lot for other people. Cancer's sensitivity and clinging emotions can upset Aquarius, who requires space for to feel free and independent. Aquarians have a detached and elusive quality about them, which other people find hard to pin down. Aquarius wants to share everything with the world and likes to be part of some sort of group. Cancer can go along with that, but is more of a private person and chooses to keep his/her feelings between the two of them. Aquarius can be unpredictable, which will disturb Cancer. They may be able to make it as lovers for a while, however a long time relationship doesn't look promising.

Cancer with Pisces

These two water signs relate to their feelings and emotions, rather than their logical mind. They are both very intuitive and will always follow their intuition before they listen to what their brain is telling them. Their vibrant imagination may sometimes run away with them and there are times when they are not sure whether they have been dreaming or if it really did happen. The good point about that is they will have the ability to dream up some amazing ideas together and make them come true. This is a very romantic and affectionate couple, with the urge to love and to be loved in return. If a conflict should occur between them, then it will be sorted out in each others arms at bed time. Together they will make an excellent team and the possibility of a happy marriage looks promising.

Leo with Leo

Two fire signs together might be compatible if they both can agree on which one of them should be the leader. These are two very strong-minded and dominating personalities. If they are going to make this union work they will both have to learn to give and take and allow the other person to shine. That should be possible, because each of them knows how important it is for their partner to be the center of attention. So one of them needs to be content with stepping back and letting the other one stand out. They could take turns doing that. Romance is high on the list for Leo, and sexually this pair will be well-suited. It will be the strongest bond in their relationship. If both of them care enough about each other and agree on sharing the limelight, then there is nothing they can't do if they are in agreement of the goal they want to reach.

Leo with Virgo

Fire sign Leo is extroverted and can be quite dominating. The earth sign Virgo is modest, reserved, and tends to be compliant. This could be a well-matched combination. Virgo's tendency to criticize may go over the head of generous Leo. Virgo, however, does appreciate Leo's humor and lovable personality. When it comes to business, extravagant Leo will do well to listen to Virgo's razor-sharp mind, because he/she has a more practical outlook on things. In their love life, Virgo may feel a bit overwhelmed by passionate Leo. Virgo will make a great effort to stimulate and please Leo. The chances for mutual pleasure and a fulfilling partnership are good, provided they appreciate the many positive qualities they both have to offer each other in their relationship.

Leo with Libra

The fire sign Leo is compatible with the air sign Libra. Both of these signs have many things in common. However, it is important for Libra to keep things balanced, so there may be times when Libra may feel extravagant, generous, and flamboyant Leo a bit over the top. Even though Leo can be bossy and dominating, Libra can get things the way he/she wants through diplomatic manipulation. Venus-ruled Libra tends to be on the emotional plane, while Leo is more sensitive. Sexually they are a good match. The Sun rules Leo and often people born under this sign bring sunshine into other people's lives with their cheerful attitude. Now and then Libra finds it hard making a decision, because they can usually see things from two sides. In situations like that, Leo will step in and take the lead. Leo pays more attention to Libra's physical appearance when it comes to lovemaking than Libra does. That is not a problem for Leo, who will soon turn Libra around. This combination could be a happy union and they should be able to share a lot of happy times together.

Leo with Scorpio

The combination of a fire sign with a water sign could turn out to be a turbulent mixture between two such powerful and strong-willed people. Their challenge would be to let go of control and make an effort not to dominate each other. You are both talented in the vicinity of the business world, as well as in the field of art. If you try hard to work together, rather than against one another, then there is no limit to what you can accomplish as a couple. Leo is frank and open-hearted, whereas Scorpio is not inclined to allow everyone into his/her secret, intense, and possessive nature. This couple may have their conflicts, but the sexual attraction is strong and their love life could prove to turn into a long-lasting relationship.

Leo with Sagittarius

This combination of fire will work well because their ruling planets, Jupiter and the Sun endow both signs with a positive and optimistic attitude. The characteristics of these two signs will bestow the couple with an open heart, forthright and generous nature. To avoid conflict, Leo needs to control his/her natural instinct to dominate the other person. Independent Sagittarius will fight back if Leo becomes too bossy or controlling, but he/she will worry and feel abandoned if Sagittarius exercises too much independence and freedom. This couple is both very sociable and loves the good life, romance, entertainment, and going out to have fun. They like meeting new people and share some of their interesting adventures with them. Both signs enjoy an active sex life. Sagittarius excites and arouses Leo, and finds that satisfying enough not to look to other horizons. This union is ideal, and promises to become a happy marriage.

Leo with Capricorn

The fire sign Leo and the earth sign Capricorn are not a good combination. These two signs are very different in nature, Leo the dazzling, flamboyant Sun child mixed with the conservative and serious Saturn-ruled Capricorn do not have much in common. In a relationship, Leo would feel too constrained. He/she would not be able to live life to the fullest like he/she enjoys so much. On the other hand, cautious Capricorn who likes to be organized and plan for the future, find it hard to understand Leo's extravagant and passionate ways. Capricorn, who is fairly reserved by nature, and refrains from showing emotions in public, can't comprehend that Leo might have needs that are not being fulfilled in their relationship. Leo craves lots of love and attention to feel appreciated. This couple have completely opposite traits, and if they were ever to indulge in a love affair, it would not last long because it would not be a happy mix.

Leo with Aquarius

While fire has a natural affinity with air, these signs are in opposition to each other in the horoscope. Although there initially may have been a physical attraction between them, when they get to know one another, they will realize the vast differences in their characters. Both signs have fixed beliefs, determination and minds of their own. They will need to be willing to cooperate and learn to find the middle ground if they are to get along. Independence means two different things to these two signs. They both like to meet other people, but Aquarius's friendliness come from more of a universal, detached point of view. Leo will not be able to understand the unpredictable antics of Aquarius. Their sexual life will not be satisfactory for Leo, because he/she can't get Aquarius's full attention. Leo needs to be admired by his/her partner, and if deprived of that Leo may think that Aquarius is uncaring. Leo might attempt to boss Aquarius, which will not work. Even though these two signs are attracted to each other initially, it is doubtful that it will work out in the long run unless there are other strong points in their horoscopes that are compatible.

Leo with Pisces

Fire sign Leo and water sign Pisces are worlds apart. Leo is a frank, open, extroverted, dazzling, and flamboyant sign. Pisces, on the other hand, has a deep, unexplained-and indescribable quality, which is not easy for the majority of people to comprehend. Leo never truly understand Pisces character. It seems to Leo that Pisces at times lives in an illusive dreamworld. When Pisces feels a bit depressed and needs a shoulder to lean on, if Leo is willing to comfort this water sign, they may be able to connect on that level, but that would have to be Leo's choice. Pisces tends to be disorganized, and that is the one thing Leo can help with. Pisces has a great admiration for Leo's determination and focus to get things done. Even though they are so different in nature, they would both benefit greatly from this connection. There is a lot they could learn from each other in ways they might never have imagined.

Virgo with Virgo

Earth with earth. Here we have a couple of like minded people. Will they be passionate lovers? This combination will be more like a passion of their mind. They are both intelligent people with a lot in common. They will always find some interesting subject to talk about. They are both very practical and like to stick to a routine. But, unless one of them has some more exciting signs or planets in the important power points in their horoscopes, they could easily get into a rut and be bored with their lives. They are quite considerate of one another and will not hassle the other person. If they can avoid getting into too much criticism of each other, then this team would stand a good chance of a happy union.

Virgo with Libra

The obvious contrast between these two signs, earth and air, is not so noticeable in this combination. Their ruling planets, Mercury and Venus, are quite compatible. These two planets have to do with the mind and emotions. They complement each other and will get on well together. They are both a bit particular in the way they organize their lives, and require some level of perfection. Libra aspires to attain balance and beauty in his/her surroundings, and are therefore, not likely to aggravate the critical side of Virgo. Socializing is important to Libra, and this sign will always have many friends. Virgo needs something to stimulate his/her mind, and if Libra can convince Virgo that their excursion will be interesting, Virgo will happily come along. Marriage is a possibility for this union.

Virgo with Scorpio

As a rule, earth is compatible with water. These two signs will work well together with the practical and the intellectual side of things. They may share the same interest in many areas. But when it comes to a love relationship, they will have difficulties, because on the emotional scale, they are very different. Scorpio has strong, intense feelings which he/she has trouble controlling sometimes. Scorpio can be demanding and will not tolerate his/her partner showing interest in the opposite sex. This person will fly off the handle in a jealous fury when provoked. Virgo, whose emotions are usually under control, will find it hard to understand that part of Scorpio. As a couple, Virgo will prove to be a trustworthy partner and generally willing to see the other person's point of view. This combination may work for a while, but unless there are other strong compatible planets in their horoscopes, this will not be a good union.

Virgo with Sagittarius

These two earth and fire signs are not a good combination. Virgo is cautious and meticulous, analyzing everything carefully. Whereas, Sagittarius thrives on excitement and new experiences. Sagittarians are very independent which gives people born under this sign a tendency to be quick, impulsive, and occasionally reckless. This is considered the happy-go-lucky sign. Sagittarius will look at life from an optimistic point of view and cannot understand why Virgo needs to be such a perfectionist and fuss small details. Virgo, on the other hand, wants a life where there is order, stability, and simplicity. He/she wants a long-term relationship, while Sagittarius may get bored and need some excitement and may find a new lover now and again. Virgo would not be too happy about that, so this relationship would never work for a long-term commitment. They would be better suited with another sign, unless other strong points in their charts are more compatible.

Virgo with Capricorn

The combinations of earth with earth will make for a stable couple with their feet on the ground. They are both realistic with a strong sense of duty and responsibilities. Virgo's ruling planet is Mercury and Capricorn is ruled by Saturn, so they are well suited for each other in the business world and in practical areas. However, they would have to learn to take time out for some fun in between their main obligations. They have to realize life is not all work and no pleasure. This couple could easily get caught up in their duties and fail to remember how important it is to nurse your feelings and take care of your emotions. Nevertheless, they are both intelligent and patient, so if any conflict should arise, they are clever enough to work it out between them. This couple should have a good foundation for a long union.

Virgo with Aquarius

There is a distinct difference between this combination of earth and air signs. The rulers of these two signs are Mercury and Uranus, and they both have a tendency to be intellectually inclined, rather than ruled by their emotions. Virgo is cautious and usually in control of his/her feelings, while Aquarius can be unpredictable and unconventional at times. But at the same time, there is definitely a unique streak running through Aquarius, and this sign is known as the greatest inventor in the zodiac. If he/she would let Virgo take care of the practical side of things, then this team could have something going for them, providing Virgo's logical mind can work out the puzzling nature of Aquarius. The sexual attraction between this couple is not strong. Virgo needs to let Aquarius mix with all the eccentric friends he/she gets involved with for there to be any hope of a long-term relationship.

Virgo with Pisces

Virgo is an earth sign and Pisces is a water sign ruled by Neptune. The earth has an affinity with water, and even though these are opposite signs, they will compliment each other. The other person might be a bit difficult to understand, because they see things in a different light. Elusive and highly intuitive Pisces will always be a mystery to logical Mercury-ruled Virgo, who analyzes everything and is guided by facts. Pisces is led by emotions and is very much in touch with their feelings, but the stability of Virgo's sensible attitude will help bring order and structure into their somewhat disorganized lives. However, Pisces will be able to add some romance and warmth to Virgo, and stir up the emotional and feeling side of him/her. Pisces need the stability of Virgo's practical outlook, and Pisces can introduce Virgo to the more imaginary side of things. If the love is there between them, then they will both benefit from this union.

Libra with Libra

When two Libra air signs gets together, there will not be any conflict whatsoever. Venus is the ruling planet of this sign. It bestows the person born under this sign with a love of peace, harmony, balance, and beauty. This couple will find it easy to agree on most things. Disagreement and dispute are very disturbing to Libra. The Libran will rather walk away from a quarrel than get involved in a heated argument. They are cheerful and easy going people, but need more of a fighting spirit for any forward development to occur. In this match, they both have an expensive and elegant taste that will be reflected in their surroundings. As a couple, their social life will probably be busy, considering they are good communicators and have lots of friends. Marriage is a probability if the love for each other is strong enough.

Libra with Scorpio

Air sign Libra and water sign Scorpio mix well together. The physical and emotional attraction between these two signs is strong. Libra has the feminine Venus as the ruling planet and Scorpio is ruled by Pluto. However, Scorpio's intensity and jealous nature may be too overpowering for gentle Libra. Scorpio is possessive and likes to keep Libra to him/herself. This can be a problem for carefree Libra, who enjoys socializing with his/her many friends, and usually strives to stay calm and balanced. The question is, can tactful Libra avoid aggravating the Scorpio's sting? If they can only agree on sharing the same interests they both enjoy, then it might strengthen the bond between them. As long as their love for one another is strong enough, they could have a good union.

Libra with Sagittarius

Air sign Libra and fire sign Sagittarius are in harmony with each other in this combination. Their ruling planets are Venus, the planet of love, and Jupiter the planet of luck. This combination will enhance their chances for a harmonious relationship that will be full of adventures. This pair knows how to enjoy life, so the possibility of a happy union is good. Libra prefers to share most things with someone special, but will be considered enough to let Sagittarius have the freedom and independence he/she finds so important. Sagittarius is fascinated by the clever way Libra manages to keep their communication on an intellectual basis. Happy-go-lucky Sagittarius will generously bestow Libra with all the little luxuries and things he/she adores. Sagittarius is frank, but often too outspoken, telling the truth without thinking it may hurt other people's feelings. If diplomatic Libra can handle that side of

Sagittarius, then they have a good chance for a successful relationship.

Libra with Capricorn

An air sign and an earth sign is not such an easy mix. So if these two signs get together, they most likely have some other important compatible planet power points in their horoscope. Capricorn is not what you would consider to be a warm, loving sign, and it would be unlikely for Libra to feel happy in a relationship without the love and affection it needs. Libra has a carefree personality and enjoys indulging in some of the luxury life has to offer. The traits of a Capricorn are associated with a serious, responsible, and ambitious nature who always strives to reach its goal. Libra would need to lavish Capricorn with an abundance of charm to get some loving attention from that work-focused partner. Libra, who adores beautiful things, would like someone to share his/her interest in the world of art, but will find it hard to pull Capricorn away from work to care about such things. This relationship would not be an ideal match, unless each party was prepared to compromise and be considerate of each other needs.

Libra with Aquarius

These two air signs complement each other. They are both friendly and take pleasure in mixing with other people. Together they would no doubt enjoy an active social life. Their love life would most certainly be warm, loving, and full of fun and games. Tactful Libra will always find a way to cope with the unpredictable nature of Aquarius. Either one of them will make major demands on the other person. Nevertheless, they can still have a close relationship, providing Libra can tolerate the freedom Aquarius requires. Libra's constant strive for balance and calmness can have a positive influence on Aquarius's impulsive antics. However, Libra rather likes that side of Aquarius, and they will most probably have some exciting adventures together. Both signs are bestowed with a sensual nature that most likely will lead to a warm, loving, and happy marriage.

Libra with Pisces

The Air sign Libra and water sign Pisces are bestowed with a certain kind of affinity for each other, even though these two elements don't usually mix. These two gentle-natured people find it easy to express their love and affection for each other. They adore the beauty of the artistic world and are both able to tune into their imagination and create a magical, romantic atmosphere. Their ruling planets, Venus and Neptune, are in harmony, and together they would be able to create some amazing things relating to the world of art. Libra's natural calmness and sense of balance will have a positive influence on Pisces, who tends to easily drift into confusion and indecision. If Libra is willing and able to lift Pisces up when he/she gets into a negative mood, then this duo could lead to a happy union.

Scorpio with Scorpio

The combination of two Scorpios from the same intense and emotional water element will make an interesting mix. They possess strong passionate feelings and desires with an unwavering stubborn nature. Scorpio does nothing by half; it is all the way or nothing. So in that respect, this couple could achieve great thing together, because they will both be so devoted to the project that they would want to see it completed to the end. However, there are likely to be some conflict, because this is two jealous people who insist getting their partner's full attention. You would think that both of them could understand where the other person is coming from and would want to compromise. But no, they both have a strong control issue and find it hard to forgive and forget. The best place to reconcile any disagreement between them are in the warmth of the bedroom. This connection is not recommended as it could turn either way – good or bad.

Scorpio with Sagittarius

This water sign and fire sign are not going to be an easy mix. Scorpio likes to be in control and is possessive of his/her partner. Sagittarius loves to feel free and independent and likes to travel and explore new adventures. Scorpio, who is jealous by nature, finds it hard to understand free-loving Sagittarius. Physically they may be attracted to each other at first and enjoy an affair, but Scorpio might kill any romance by being demanding and trying to control Sagittarius, who will probably run as far away as possible. Scorpio can appear mystical by being secretive and not revealing everything he thinks or feels. This might confuse Sagittarius, who is naturally frank and open. This duo does not have much in common, and a long-term relationship is not recommended unless they both have compatible planets in some of the power points of their horoscopes.

Scorpio with Capricorn

Water mixes well with earth. The ruling planets of these two signs are Pluto and Saturn. So this promises to be a good combination. When it comes to serious business, this duo would work. In a case where both have a common goal, either at their job or in a business situation, the two of them would be committed to the project and determined to finish it together. In a loving relationship, possessive Scorpio would not have to worry if Capricorn should look for another outlet, as he/she would be pleased with this reliable partner. Providing they don't get into any conflicts, this should be a good team. With sensual Scorpio's ability to highlight their sex life, and Capricorn's resilience and endurance, this could be a successful marriage.

Scorpio with Aquarius

Here we have two strong willed signs. Water sign Scorpio and air sign Aquarius ruled by Pluto and Uranus. Aquarius, the universal lover of the zodiac who enjoys being friendly with many people, will clash with possessive Scorpio, who wants a partner to him/herself. However, if they could agree on working towards a mutual goal, great achievement would be possible. With Aquarius's vivid imagination and Scorpio's powerful driving force, the result might end up with an amazing accomplishment. Also, if they apply this side of their character in their love life, they may both hear bells ringing. Anyway, Aquarius will probably be put off by Scorpio's control issues. Scorpio's jealous nature would upset Aquarius's unpredictable moods and the need to be involved with different kinds of social groups. Unless there is a compatibility aspect between some of the other power points in their horoscopes, then this will not be a good match.

Scorpio with Pisces

These two water signs, Scorpio and Pisces, are ruled by Pluto and Neptune. There is a magical attraction between these two signs, and their relationship will be rather intense and emotional. Scorpio's natural instinct to dominate might lead him/her to think Pisces has surrendered to his/her wishes, but that might just be an act. Pisces has an ability to calm Scorpio's inner tensions and obsessive nature. Both signs are bestowed with strong intuition and will sense the moods of the other person. They both tend to overreact if things go wrong or a disagreement crop up between them. Their emotions seem to blur the facts, which prevent the matter from getting resolved. They share a deep interest in the mystical and the supernatural world. As lovers they are a perfect match and any kind of long-term relationship promises to be successful.

Sagittarius With Sagittarius

This combination of two fire signs will be a vigorous one. They are both ruled by Jupiter. They are two optimistic people born under the same sign, which is considered the happy-go-lucky sign. They will probably be on the go most of the time, busy creating an exciting life for themselves. Life will never be dull for this couple. They will always have some kind of adventure to look forward to. As lovers, they would have fun and keep an open mind. Freedom and independence are important to both of them, and the danger here is that they might drift apart. Unless they can agree to share similar interests, adventures, and fun together, then this duo might slowly glide away from each other. There would have to be some strong compatible points in their horoscopes for this connection to last.

Sagittarius With Capricorn

The obvious difference between a fire sign and an earth sign is obvious in this duo. Sagittarius is ruled by Jupiter, the planet of expansion. Saturn the serious planet of limitation is the ruler of Capricorn. Sagittarius, who is a happy-go- lucky sign, is frank and open-minded, but restless by nature. Capricorn is conservative, cautious, and careful. This is a determined, responsible, and hard working person. Whereas, Sagittarius likes to go on a venture now and again, where he/she can discover new things and meet people. Ambitious Capricorn needs to be working towards reaching a goal. Sagittarius is carefree and sometimes like to act like the big player. Their love life will most likely be unsatisfying and will not help them create a lasting bond. Unless other planetary combinations in their horoscopes are compatible, this is not going to be a good mix. However, if they can overcome their differences, then these two signs have a lot to offer and learn from each other.

Sagittarius With Aquarius

There is a strong connection between fire and air. Sagittarius is the fire sign and Aquarius the air sign. Their ruling planets are Jupiter and Uranus. These two signs have a strong influence on each other and will inspire each other intellectually. They both attract many unusual and unique people. These are two friendly signs who need lots of friends and acquaintances in their lives. However, both signs love their independence and need to feel free to enjoy their own space. Therefore, they are willing to give the other person the space they need. Aquarius takes a lot of pleasure in being involved in groups where they can make lots of friends, while Sagittarius likes to dabble in different kinds of investments where he/she is often lucky to gain a win. They have many things in common and their values are similar. Both are great at using their imagination when it comes to their love life. This union stands a good chance for a successful marriage.

Sagittarius With Pisces

The combination of fire and water with these two signs will not be an easy one, but there could be a potential for some kind of relationship. Their ruling planets are Jupiter and Neptune. Among their commonalities are an appreciation for the worlds of philosophy, religion, mysticism, charitable causes, travel, and being involved in humanitarian organizations. On the other hand, for some couples born under these signs it might mean there will be times when they feel confused or undecided. Pisces can withdraw and live a private life where he/she will imagine the worst when his/her partner gets the urge to adventure out on an independent trip. Sagittarius is a generous sign and has many good attributes. However, love and tender care is not one of them, and he/she is also frank and outspoken, sometimes with a sharp tongue, which would hurt hypersensitive Pisces. By nature, Sagittarius is active, quick, efficient, and well organized, whereas Pisces is just the opposite. This sign is indecisive, impractical, and disorganized. They may connect as lovers for a while, but it doesn't look promising for a long-term relationship.

Capricorn with Capricorn

These two Capricorn earth signs are sure to share similar values. They both have a cautious and conservative outlook on life. Despite agreeing on most things they tend to be too serious and wrapped up in ambitions while they reach for their goal. Some more cheerful and lighthearted people need to come into their lives or they will become bored with each other. If this duo is working on the same project, to ensure they get a successful result, they would be wise to get some outside inspiration to help their interest stay fresh and alive. They each have a stubborn streak in their nature, so to avoid any rift between them, they need to keep their partnership as a business one, rather than as lovers. This is not the best combination for a loving relationship. Each partner needs a happier and more jovial person as their companion.

Capricorn with Aquarius

Practical, earth sign Capricorn ruled by serious Saturn, and Uranus, ruled Aquarius, is an air sign. These two signs will need to go through many changes for for them to build a good partnership. They both have a stubborn side to their personalities and are very much into their own way of handling life. Capricorn needs a secure, stable life and finds it hard to change to Aquarian ways. Unpredictable, unorthodox Aquarius is creative and likes to experiment with some of his/her new and exciting way-out original ideas. On the other hand, Capricorn is determined to stick to the same plan he/she decided to follow to reach the goal he/she is aiming at. Capricorn likes to be financially secure and would try to inflict his sensible attitude onto Aquarius. This might be a hard lesson for Aquarius to learn. For this duo to have any kind of relationship they would both need to bend some of their standards a bit. It would be good for Capricorn to learn to loosen up a little, and Aquarius to pick up some of the important values Capricorn can teach.

Capricorn with Pisces

Earth signs go well together with water signs, even though these two people are quite different in many ways. Capricorn is ruled by the planet Saturn, and Pisces is ruled by Neptune. Capricorn can bring stability to Pisces dreamy and imaginary world and he/she can quite easily adapt to the safety and security that Capricorn provides. Capricorn might not be able to fulfill Pisces emotional needs for a romantic partner. Pisces may feel rejected and wounded by Capricorn's unwillingness to show any warm feelings. Pisces is a hypersensitive sign and not at all inclined to be competitive, so he/she is not a threat in any way to Capricorn, who can then go about his business and follow the plan he has laid out for reaching a long-time goal. Practical Capricorn is well-organized and can help to bring order and structure into Pisces somewhat disorganized life. If Pisces can appeal to Capricorn's hidden feeling and draw out the softer side of him/her, then there is a good possibility that this union could be a successful one.

Aquarius with Aquarius

These two Aquarius air signs are completely suited for each other. If Venus is placed in a compatible position in each other's horoscope, then they will have a great love life filled with many personal interests and original ideas. They are both impulsive, and it might surprise them that their partners act like that because that is usually their own way of operating. This is not a couple who dwells deeply into things. If any conflict should arise between them, they would not allow themselves to become resentful or go into moodiness for long periods of time. This pair is ruled by Uranus, which bestows on them an unconventional nature. Aquarius's friendliness come from a more universal, detached point of view. They are the humanitarians of the zodiac and care a lot for other people. Providing there are other compatible planets in the power points in their horoscopes, then this duo should have a happy and promising relationship together.

Aquarius with Pisces

These two signs are not a good match, because they are so different in their temperaments. Aquarius is an air sign ruled by the original, inventive, erratic, unpredictable, unorthodox planet, Uranus, while hypersensitive Pisces's ruling planet is Neptune, which has to do with mystery and illusion. None of these two signs could reform to live by the rules and limitations of the planet Saturn, therefore, they go beyond everyone's normal boundary and display unique qualities to the amazement of other people. They both possess an out of the ordinary personality that is different from anyone else. There might be times when they both feel at odds with other people unless they are of the same signs. However, as a couple they may not be so compatible. This sign needs the security of a partner who constantly assures the emotional Pisces that he/she is loved. Aquarius likes to feel free to mix with many different friends. Their love life might be complex. Pisces will find it hard to understand Aquarius's lighthearted attitude to sex and would most probably retreat to live a private and seclusive lifestyle. This is not a good combination that will last long.

Pisces with Pisces

Two water signs together would generate an emotional relationship. However, there would be a lot of understanding between these two people who are gifted with amazing imaginations. Both of these individuals are bestowed with some special qualities, and one would give way to the other and lend a shoulder to cry on when the hypersensitive side of Pisces hurts. As lovers, they would understand each other's needs. In fact, they would sense what the other person wants. Pisces is a highly intuitive sign. They can have dreams and come out of them with some far-fetched original ideas. Between the two of them, they would be able to create some fantastic pieces of art or write a great novel. The problem they would need to overcome would be to decide what to paint or what story to start, because they would have several ideas in mind. But once they get organized and started to work on a project, the confusion would disappear and give way for their dream to become a reality. This promises to be a successful relationship.

The End

Thank you for purchasing my book. I hope you enjoyed it and that you learned some valuable information from it and gained a better understanding of the characteristic of not only yourself, but also of your family and friends. If you enjoyed it, please write a review for it on Amazon. Let me know your thoughts and feedback, so I can continue to write books and please my readers.

My website

http://astrologymadesimpleandeasy.com/

Other Books by Hanne Klein

Astrology Made Simple and Easy to Understand

Doorways To Astrology

Jupiter The Planet Of Luck And Good Fortune In Your Horoscope

The Zodiac Signs In Great Details

Follow me on Facebook

About the Author

Hanne Klein is an astrologer who has studied astrology for about 30 years. Using astrology, she has made personal and business charts for many people, assisting them to observe their strengths, showing them where and how they could use astrology to enhance their lives.

She is also an author and an illustrator. She loves writing and has written four astrology books. 'Doorways To Astrology' and 'Astrology Made Simple And Easy To Understand,' which has been on the best seller list for a long time. The third astrology book is 'Jupiter The Planet Of Luck And Good Fortune In Your Horoscope.' The latest book is 'The Twelve Zodiacs Signs In Great details.'

She also loves drawing cartoons and people and has illustrated three of her books with cute cartoons.

Astrology is an excellent tool. It teaches you about your gifts, talents and the path you are best suited to follow.

Hanne is married and has a family.